CRUELLY YOURS

The element of CRUELTY in human affairs

The problem of humanity
is that it sees itself too
kindly; which it isn't.

Pradeep PK Maheshwari

CRUELLY YOURS

The element of Cruelty in Human affairs

The problem of humanity is that it sees itself too kindly; which it isn't.

By Pradeep PK Maheshwari

Available as ebook : (on kindle)
https://www.amazon.in/dp/B08V4XG7Q4

Feedback: gururdeva@yahoo.com

Introduction

I come from the Sri Aurobindo Ashram in Pondicherry and have noticed humanity needs to take an evolutionary step towards a more expansive consciousness to rise above its present predicaments that it is bogged down in.
For now it is a slow progress in a spiral which seems to be history and humanity repeating itself over and over. There are thousands of books on the principles of spiritual emancipation as talked about in Indian Vedic philosophy but rarely does anyone explain the baby steps to be taken by a novice average Joe and why and REALATED MORE TO THE PRESENT state of affairs, conditions, prevalent thinking and practices and more... something the average guy in the street can immediately relate to.

I have personally worked hard to develop my intuitive abilities along with language command so that I can say precisely what I am trying to say and what I am seeing in the ensemble of things in regard to the forces at work in this world and manifestations it appears in.

I was always been a bit of a recluse. I had created a smoke screen of man about town but rarely involved and avoided disturbance & interference if I could avoid it. I am opening up for my daughter specially and other children/cousins so that before this lamp goes out I have passed on what I have learnt from my direct experience of life. Of course what is happening in the world is out there for all to see. I am being called negative but then it is easy to call realists as pessimists. I do feel that the cruel side of human nature has been always more prominent than the better side in proportion of 70:30.

Humanity has many words and explanations to cover up its known negative emotional state; something that is nowadays called to be in "DENIAL". We have enough cleverness to know what is not good and needs to be hidden. Deceit and cunning is in-built in our machinations. We are deeply aware of it as can be seen in the philosophical and religious treatises around but we prefer to explain it away in a million ways.

My only point when I speak out is that humanity needs to get out of this denial aspect so that we can all bask in the basic goodness that there is in this world and maximize it.

Unfortunately what I have seen is that given an opportunity, social conditions permitting people do permit their cruel, negative side to emerge and take advantage of the situation.

I have been talking a lot on this aspect lately. Mainly because I feel in the present time this tendency is raising its head in a vigorous way. Technology and the tools now available to us have made inflicting hurt, propagating our desires and spreading our tentacles real easy.

I am not the only one. Read this: "Of all tyrannies, a tyranny sincerely exercised for the good of its victims may be the most oppressive. It would be better to live under robber barons than under omnipotent moral busybodies. The robber baron's cruelty may sometimes sleep, his cupidity may at some point be satiated; but those who torment us for our own good will torment us without end for they do so with the approval of their own conscience." — C. S. Lewis

We need to really wake up to this before we have destroyed the planet and our habitat and ourselves.

The Mind: the artist.

There is no way an indoctrinated and conditioned mind can shift its own mess to find its lies. It simply is not designed that way nor does it have any tools.

The very nature of the mind is that all it has is all important and meaningful. All else is false.

Once the mind has aligned with the truth it has to go into hiding because the rest of the world would otherwise burn it at the stake.

The foundation of this world is based on misconstructions. The problem if any as you say will be corrected when the element of sincerity and honesty enters the human consciousness.

You are barking until then at the wrong tree.

But people, honest people, see some of the dishonesty going around and on which life is based and they are wanting to make this aware to others. It is wastage of time; like adding a spoonful of fresh water to the sea. It does add to one's sense of superiority though.

Yes it keeps on creating images inside our heads and we think that we are part of the Reality and we see clearly the Reality that has been formed in our minds which of course must be what we are noticing and sensing through all our senses.

We start seeing things correctly on when we take on a dispassionate disposition. For example a man in love simply sees nothing but what he wants to see in his beloved. There is even a phrase that Love is blind.

The attachments we have make us blind to things we do not want to see and glorify everything we do want to see. This is the reason our judgments are mostly in error about others and a lot of everyday things that we assume and act upon. Tragic consequences are an everyday occurrence.

Similarly we can see ogres and demons or Divine and God. Our analysis is therefore always in error.

The first step is to accept this fact. Our cussedness and misplaced pride is the bar. The curtains then start falling away.

We have been deciphering the world will show us how we have been in error earlier and will continue to be so.

We have been accepting what is taught us without question. They even have a name for it: Conditioning.

All this is understood but we merrily create new worlds in our head and blithely plod on.

This is the reason for death. The reality we create is non-sustainable. We have been cleverly using this as an excuse to do away with those we do not see in alignment with our goals of supremacy – down from the Emperor to the hoodlum in the street.

And LIFE on Earth is VAAAst enough to embrace all little eccentricities.

So is it possible that when parents have children they are thinking more of their own old age and pensions instead of the pleasure of having a child and help the child to create a new future thru him? I don't think they are thinking so.

The whole act starts in selfishness and ends in selfishness. Children are means to an end. There is an attachment but mostly it is again founded in selfishness.

Yet we expect the world to grow into a wonderful new creation full of love, kindness and compassion.

My father never shared a single thought or fear of his with me. It was always a "senior-junior" relationship like in an office. He was doing his duty and I was expected to do mine though none ever told what was expected of me and why or even there ever being a hint as to how to go about it.

He never talked about anything or helped me understand what was being seen by me and put my thinking on the right track.

The only sentence I remember him by is "No. It would be better this way….".

But they, my parents were talking about me to all others and complaining most of the time. What a trail of dislike and disempowerment they left for me. It was a cruel thing to do but they were lauded while I was derided on their tell-tale stories. Why" Because I was not behaving by their rules and as expected of a child. Wherever needed embellishments were added to the story to make it special I suppose and their troubles would seem insurmountable – they were, as I see it and understand now, laying the ground for themselves as not being responsible.

Of course a crane had left me on the doorstep and a burden added to their lives by somebody called god.

And of course they did their best as all parents always do for the good of their children.

I distinctly carry the feeling that I was unwanted, not really a pleasure and as a mini adult quite a burden to carry which in their minds they did wonderfully.

I simply never counted. On seeing around I see this about describes the entire cultural ethos in which a large swathe of Indian children are brought up in. Nothing is taught. Nothing is explained. They are sent to school of sorts and (NB: our schools are really not worth talking about as formative institutions of excellence) in the most part the parent's job is done.

The feeling I have always got is that children are "Ce sont des inattendus"….. they happen.

Neither is their birth planned nor their life nor their future given much thought. The life path is simple. Get a Diploma and job and start your own family. In the meanwhile go out and play and leave the parents alone but be ready to take care of them when they are old.

To me this is extreme cruelty. The parents are laying the foundations for an unhappy tortured life. Nobody knows how to stop this chain. And this is what this book is all about.

Can we teach them?

I remember over 40 years ago when I came to settle in Delhi while on my regular way to take my French Language classes at 8 am I would see on the way a Buddhist novice lama. When I first saw him he was in full vigour. You could see in his eyes the excited enlightened mind of a fully armed "MIND" with knowledge of the monasteries going forth to impress and bring wisdom to the world in some quick easy steps. His arrogance could be inferred from the fact that he was staying in the center of the road and in opposite direction of the traffic as if he was above all these frumperies of the human kind.

Gradually over the year I saw him a little tired, walking slower and on the side of the road.

Soon he stopped being seen.

I saw him again some years later, all tired, walking slowly, visibly old and burdened with the hardship of life as a monastic in a city that would never care.

Fatigue was written on his face.

Did I imagine defeat too?

People who have been brushed off or hurt by another take a merited dislike of the perpetrator. While the perpetrator goes on unhindered in his life and flourishing. This rankles deeply. When we continue to receive news of how well he is flourishing and enjoying life while we simper and fret in our corners we can only feel and think of karma and how it should be hurting them back and we are surprised that the sky is not falling on their heads and their pants are not catching fire.

It is very rare to see anyone calling upon oneself extra "pain" because this helps in opening up and breaking the shackles.

But it is a process that we can see and for example we have all these ascetics gone before us and some can be seen around us even in modern life if we have the eyes to see them.

I remember talking to my Guardian in the Ashram and telling him that I felt I was growing in width but not depth. But he was not the kind who would wont to tell me what to do and show others the way. Instead he asked me what did I think was the solution.

I replied to him that I seem to manage well in life and quite able to manage my affairs so just yet do not see anything able to hold me back and this is my weakness; the only way I can see is by restricting myself by marriage but this I was really not interested in as I was seeing all around me nothing but strife in married life but then perhaps that is what I needed - but then I said I am too young to get into that trap just now.

Marriage proposals were coming thru family and friendly contacts. As I study numerology, I saw that my nemesis is a number 8 as it would my diametrically opposite and if I could learn to live in harmony with this number, I being a 6 my emancipation is assured.

But life seemed beautiful only with another number 6. I had six memorable affairs but none of the ladies would agree to marriage. The ladies with number 8 ladies were always eager to go along with me though. I resisted all pressures from life to get married to a number 8

Then suddenly life changed and turned upside down. I was left with no options. The only option I had left was building a home or run away into the forest. I am not the running away kind.

I had one option left to me and I was very disinclined to take it. I was in a quandary. This option would have given me relative safety to pursue my Sadhana but relationship wise I would be walking on pins and nettles. I was tied down by life like a goat and I said to myself "well boy, how long will you run away from the inevitable?"

Finally I realised that this is what is written for me and eventually I put all cares in the hands of my Gurudev and married at the advanced age of 46.

I am glad to say the real Sadhana took off like a rocket. It was also the most contrary experience I seem to have had in this and past lives. The flood gates of all that was being closeted, hidden, controlled opened. There I was standing in front of myself, entirely exposed and had to learn to live all over again. But I plodded on using all the wisdom and friendly assistance available to me. The break through took 20 years in coming.

I now realise that it could not have been otherwise. Running away as humanity does cannot be a solution.

Sarangha Kay

At least we should know what is witchcraft, what is angelic and what is original. Then at least we can understand the so called "world" better. But what is my agenda? Well to be frank my agenda is not to fall into dark occult just because I do not qualify for higher orthodoxy;

is celibacy the thing?

Pradeep Pk Maheshwari

Celibacy, the physical act may be forcefully stopped but the act continues in the mind and the body responds and becomes disturbed. The thought that celibacy will take us to God is an idiotic concept that only the simple mind can envisage - not knowing better. Something like the idea that flapping arms or adding wings to arms will make us fly.

You are only being cruel to your body and yourself. Eventually this frustration and pain my also give rise to cruel actions and thereby others that enjoin with you as partners will suffer too.

Yes but when you start entering first the intuitive mind and later see the connect of the body with the other mental states your focus of interest changes. Often the thought arrives that all this coupling first needs insincere wooing, playing second fiddle to somebody else's vanity and then organising the body positions to go about the act etc are to say the least CUMBERSOME and fraught with dangers like society's displeasure, disease and loss of self-control to boot.

But voluntary and loving sex can be an eye opener to one's own "self" as the wooing requires self-control and discipline.

There is a lot of exchange of VITAL energies and this is generally speaking highly important and required to make the existential experience whole.

One of these days when humanity begins to think and wonder, they will see how we docilely permitted the pharma to sing its song because our minds could not cross beyond the "safety" part.

How could the earthlings ever imagine that they were not connected to Mother nature and would not be affected by their activities. We have actually created new illnesses and grossly inflated others by our industrial activities in which the big pharma also falls.

Our simple minds easily construed that if we could keep the weather out by creating a wall and roof, we can also create walls against viruses!

Against this thinking lies the knowledge of medicine from the last thousands of years which has been conveniently allowed to be forgotten.

The music is now metal. The food is processed. The light is electronic. The drugs are synthetic.

The emotions are pretend. Cruelty to each other is real.

The thinking is non-existent.

For now this is the world.

But soon, soon when we have exhausted the options and the music has jarred on our nerves to make us revolt and the food has blocked our chemistry and we see death all around us, we shall recognize the error and rebirth will appear.

The easier we make for them, the more engrossed they get in in expanding their operations to repeat their pleasurable activities.

Never, ever does the mind goes towards the idea, that given these possibilities, "what am I doing here stuck in this groove?" Let us think big and bigger. Let us think of all the things that need improvement and let us work on improving them.

That is where the fun is. Kill two birds with one stone. Improve conditions and future possibilities and enjoy it too.

The speed with which we condemn, reject or accept is astounding, incorrect and most of the time we come to the wrong, rather opposite conclusion; as if a small demon were sitting there and manipulating our thinking process.

No wonder we have more wars than handshakes.

I give this as an example how our minds can twist things to fit I with their purpose.

Take this quote that I wrote.

"Our digestive systems have gone all down the drain.

Our bodies are suffering from malnutrition as the system is not absorbing/assimilating all that we are eating.

EATING MORE and BETTER things is not the answer."

Immediately I received this response: [If eating better is not the answer, can you tell me a way to make our bodies healthy?]

My answer is self-explanatory:

"I used the term Eating Better Things.

Eating better is not the same as eating better things.

Eating better in my view is eating things that the body already recognizes and can process. Stay as natural as Mother Nature designed it. Even good food can be destroyed in the cooking and processing so understand this part too.

There are individual sad stories. Millions of them. Half a dozen each for all of us at least. This world is not designed for just pleasure and fun.

I talk of universal psyche trends. You need to also take that into account. The present will change a little and the needle on the record will circle will go on moving but by not letting the focus dwell on the Universal and bringing the change at psyche level, nothing will change now or in the future.

By focusing on individual stories we stop the more evolutionary thoughts and waves to catch momentum and establish in the human consciousness.

The sadist side in humanity is out on parade.

The cruel side of humans, subdued and suppressed due to social factors is now out in the open and the digital is helping it spread and hide in the open.

Malachy Matthews

12 Gardai. Some armed. Against One man with a knife? Nobody knows his troubles. Shoot him in the legs if needed. Surely a better way to disarm him than shooting to kill? On the other hand a Garda may have made a mistake in the heat of the moment and will have to live with that for the rest of his life. Rather dead than live with that?

Pradeep Pk Maheshwari

What kind of "Heat of the Moment" is this?

You are being too kind.

They are being trained that way. They are conditioned to shoot first and ask questions afterwards.

In a lot of cases I say it is best. The beasts stopped for all time because the democratic/social process only ends up feeding them in full comfort or ever and ever in the name of due legal process.

The administration is no kind god looking after us.

The same mentality as of the Lords of 1000 years ago and the slave owners of 2000 years ago is still floating around.

You don't matter or matter just about to pay regular taxes so that they can flourish in their mansions.

Wake up.

Want a Better Year?

Learn this trick to confuse Destiny.

Let this year be of striving and not simply complaining.

WE need solutions and we need to run away from airing grouses as if our duty is done when we have delineated the problem and blamed somebody for it and then sit back saying that "there is nothing that can be done" .

When we look back we shall see that somewhere we were, with our attitudes part of the problem.

To progress these things are to be kept in mind and applied in our lives:

Study the question from all angles; specially from the angles we do not want to see as it points to ourselves.

When we see the answers, we need to keep them in the forefront of our memories by writing it down and looking at it everyday first thing in the morning to remind our subconscious and eventually make it a new habit of thinking and doing things.

I call this the reminder list.

As a trick it works!!!

40 years ago one niece of mine had a boy. The day we met it was a collision of interest. He would not go to anybody after that, do nothing without me and in my arms was absolutely an angel incarnate. Why did this happen when in the perception of people I am ruff and gruff type?

Aruna my daughter has been the most wonderful experience. The bond of child in repose in her father's care with no qualms is a feeling of great sustenance to the spirit of the father.

This kind of absolute affection is not seen in adults though I have experienced it only once. The adults should meditate on this...why?

My dearest and life-worth-living-moments are when my children hug me and want to be hugged back.

When I see children I want to hug them all and let them play with my beard but parents today are so "Barriered" that no one can approach anyone anymore.

But I have some experiences that are worth noting because these happened in enclosed spaces where the other parents felt safe.

1) I was taking a small 22 seater plane with 17 French tourists (some time in the 1970s). Along with was a mother with a child in her arms and all the bags that normally go with a child. As a matter of normal decency, I took the child in my arms, the mother did not resist and the child came willingly. Bug the Frenchies got all worked up. One woman even later came to me and forced me to return the child to the mother - she was so upset - "what kind of a mother allows another to take the child so?" was her complaint.

My thoughts: We are in a plane for god's sake high up in the sky - I am not going away anywhere!

2) Again a plane, a young couple was having problems calming their 3-4 year old girl down who was afraid for her doll. So I took matters in hand. Talked to the child showed her how the seat belt is tied and how to include the doll. I kept the child engaged and the flight went well for all of us.

3) We were going to Paris (2018) by train there were only 5 people in the compartment. A mother was with her baby and obviously not exactly happy. I tried to talk to the boy but he did not respond much as he was evidently not used to other people. But I talked a little to the mother and went and sat with my people. Suddenly the woman got up,

put the child in my lap and went to the toilet without a word. I kept the child busy and engaged and went for a walk with it talking to it all the time. No trouble at all.

Some years ago when looking for clothing for Aruna a lady with a child in her arms was also in the shop. The child saw me and jumped into my arms. Thankfully the mother let it which nowadays is unusual.

I love these moments

A little Occult Psychology for today.

Humans are normally a mixture of tendencies. The Basic "Being or Soul" as humans call it in many individuals often is a full-fledged demon who enters the baby's atmosphere at or just before birth. These people later prove to be cruel, hard-hearted and with little or no empathy or sympathy. They will twist everything in their favour and blame others. They never see any good in anyone, always ascribe malevolent intentions to others to justify their own conclusions and misbehavior.

They are nice enough on the outside and in general but their origins can be recognised by one specific behaviour: They CANNOT BE in error. You are not to speak ill of them or find anything wrong in the slightest. This brings out the dragon in a very destructive, flame throwing, vindictive manner.

Normally they are intelligent and clever enough to understand that this world can hurt them back so they try to go along with the society they are in, they are good workers but given some authority or power or money, they cannot hold themselves back and just allow themselves to be what they are wherever they know they can get away with it (only there).

They will go along with you only if it is in their interest and so do not make good reliable friends because they tend to lie, distort stories and narratives so obviously that people are scared away from them.

I have known too many for comfort but then it seems I seem to attract them in some way. To deal with them requires a greater level than normal of understanding of human nature and self-discipline to not get involved in their provocative methods.

From the human angle, I have observed that they seem to be closely aligned to number 8 in this material world.

This is good as you are doing Raj Yoga under pressure it is good for your own spiritual growth and should be seen as a help from above.

We talk of sharing

But demand that permission be taken at every step.

We talk of spontaneous love but build barbed wire fences around us.

I eat my orange.

You eat your orange.

You make your marmalade and use your own spoon.

You will not partake of mine.

I have really no wish to share either my orange or my company and my space not at all.

The child knows not these limits.

It can get vile out there for a child of 70 like me.

Basically we are looking for justification from society.

On our own we are "nothing".

Most people are quite happy with their state of being because they have convinced themselves of their innate goodness/kindness/greatness.

You'll be surprised to know how many (99.9% of them) really believe in what they are doing. And from their talk it is obvious that they are doing it always with a greater good in mind.

They see themselves as kind and serving a Divine purpose. And worse they go about telling the world how to be kind and helpful.

The parent blowing his top at the child.

The husband hurting the wife.

The teacher punishing the student.

The doctors doing their bit.

The judges interpreting the law.

The executioner beheading people.

Intuition simply opens you to all round information floating in the Universe and to the basic truth that we shall never know the details of each and every incident.

And this is where the point of contention is. People want the TRUTH they say. This is an error of use of the word truth. What they want are the intimate details of an incident/gossip. (I would first ask them: "WHY at all?")

And for this there is no way of knowing unless you have passed way further than the intuitive into knowledge of the past, present and future - into the omniscient.

Why are there no lessons on as to how to treat rogues, vagabonds, narcissists and scammers who are trying to take something from you?

Why do I have to be nice and kind because I am so?

Doesn't wisdom ask us to deal with the situation as the situation demands?

Just in passing I thought I'll mention my philosophy on reading.....

On reading:

After a certain amount of reading, it is best to stop reading and observing and living life in the way our spirit commands us. I would say 5000 books in a lifetime is more than enough.

Otherwise we only confuse ourselves with great amount of data that is actually dead data as it is never going to be used...cannot be used for obvious reasons.

Too much reading means associating with the thoughts of others and it impedes the development of our personal INTUITION.

Shannon Lee McGillion

I had to fly last week & yes they sardines us in a plane
(some � seats were left empty though)

 Pradeep PK Maheshwari.

This is the truth of the last century. For maximum profit
and ease of reach the concept in force has been of that of
"Sardining". See how the city blocks and the mega
apartment structures have been planned. New York is the
finest example. Buildings in close proximity going up to
50+ floors at least. The drainage required to service all
these people are not adequate. The centration of
population is totally unhealthy. Breeze cannot flow thru
this conglomeration. It is like a cancerous git/boil on
mother earth. We have created like our concentrated
"capsules" in medicine, islands and tin/cement boxes of
misery.

We need to spread out. Now that we can travel with ease
and communicate at long distances, why are we so blocked
on thinking of still living life of dead sardines?

So, what is a "problem"....how do you call something a problem?

What constitutes a problem?

Are you unhappy with this world?

Do you wish to change this world?

And you are not being able to change things as your thinking ordains so you see it all as a problem.

The world has been flowing on since millions of years. Did it see the living beings on its surface making a mess and considered it a problem?

What did it do?

It slowly, gradually without ever being perturbed, instituted changes and things just flowed on.

Perhaps the only problem is that we want it to happen NOW!

My experience is that most poor can blame their fate/parents to give them a bad start and do so and remain clogged at that point for the rest of their lives.

Even if they find some to help them they rarely allow a helping hand to reach them as they have to contend with their pride that blocks movement, communication and trust.

They do not have the aspiration required to get out of the mud either. They believe in this socialism atmosphere that things should be handed out to them as a right.

Their intelligence, education and training not being adequate they are unable to grasp the seriousness of their situation until long later when their physical strength abates and so does the source of any income.

The rich often when rich by inheritance blow away their wealth for the same reason.

And they all crowd their lives by taking the burden of wife and children when they themselves are not ready to take the weight of their own lives.

In the war of life we would all be rather NON-Combatants.

We all want to enjoy the peace but make little effort to bring peace into war torn areas of life.

We talk of humility but behave with arrogance which can be seen in three dimensional show-off actions in virtually everything we do.

We talk of sharing but accumulate everything we can as if the "supply" might stop tomorrow.

We talk of crowding but keep on adding to the number of floors.

We talk of greenhouse gases but at the personal level contribute nothing to reduce it.

The worst show of our basic attitude comes out in the patronage we are giving to SUV which has mostly no justification in the element of transportation as a necessity.

We ARE the Enemy.

Death is not a punishment. It is a release.

The verdict of death has served to terrorise the public into submission to the governing forces or the conquering forces. It is sign of the inherent cruelty of man to overwhelm the psychology of the living by firmly implanting fear.

Humans are very strong when it comes to accusing others. We lie most of the time. Framing others comes to us as easily as abc.

The judiciary and the judicial system is heavily influenced by the say-so of people that they call witnesses. Assuming that everyone is honest is the biggest lie being perpetrated on Earth. It is a huge clear sign of how we live in an illusionary world of our making.

I remember seeing the movie Papillon (from the book Papillon – a real story of the prison system in the colonies that all government had in the 18/19th centuries) in which the graphic image of a man struggling to avoid death by guillotine is impressed in my mind. What was he struggling for? The life that had been dished out to him was it worth living? Then why did he rebel and invite death upon his head? How come he was not seeing it as a welcome release from this cruel and impossible incarceration?

What is it in us that makes us so cruel? Just go back to some simple manifestations of our cruelties and you will understand how we bring it out in the name of religion and doing "good". Two examples will suffice: The Inquisition and the Hitlerian Final Solution.

The other everyday manifestations are Rapes because the woman was

"instigating" it by provoking the hormones of the man. The robberies because the man was showing off his wealth… The mother-in-law making life hell for the daughter in law because she felt the control and power over her son ebbing… The step parent ruining a child's life… The neighbors accusing their brethren out of jealousy…And the worst: accusing one's child of running one's life by taking birth which is so glaringly not the child's fault.

But the cruelest manifestation is the part that all this is tolerated by the people and society as a whole as normal part of being human and correct. The vilest gossip is received with glee. The courts accept accusations basing it on the theory that no-one would lie out of spite and there is no good reason for lying anyway.

How on earth with lying so prevalent did humans accept the promulgation that humans are basically honest and kind when effectively we know, all of us, by experience that it is not so.

We rarely go deep into studying the accusations to understand the vile motivations that inspire us. Yet we label ourselves as HUMANE that we certainly aren't but fortunately in individual acts in small measures it is to be found spread out like stars in the night sky but unfortunately not bright enough to create "DAY".

Grow and let grow.

I hide nothing from my children and younger family members and from friends not at all.

I think parents make a great mistake by not taking their children into their confidence and not sharing about the world. They need to know about the ground realities - truthfully so they can plan ahead with accuracy.

What I have tried to make them see is that even with all the negativity in life, something beautiful can be made out of it. We should look for solutions and work at them for resolution.

I have taught my daughter to learn to live with it by tuning herself and taking care of certain defects in ourselves. etc etc I have never allowed personal animosity to sour my relationships though I am hurting inside and things could have been so more beautiful but well we do what we can and must do it.

By being on FB my instructions reach them indirectly IF they are reading any of it. This way they do not feel personally attacked/criticised. They can see that I am saying whatever I wish to say to everybody. If it applies to anyone of them and it is not right then one needs to learn and do something about it.

Moreover I have peer review from you all so that it becomes easier for the children to accept the philosophy more easily, soulfully and open heartedly.

I have no private life to hide and try to give a distinct flavor of honesty, caring and tolerance. It has taken a whole life to arrive at this point

We open our eyes and we find ourselves in a body and in a world. Nothing is really ours. We seem to have no choices.

All decisions are being taken and soon we get into the habit of letting things happen.

We blumber along with one day following another.

We do realise that we are not good enough for the ensemble of life surrounding us but something inside will not admit it. We put up a show and charade that is out to prove - "It shows off that I am living under inhuman conditions and maintaining my superior air nevertheless. It shows how tolerant I am although I know exactly what is wrong. It shows that I am busy doing all that can be done to keep the society going and at an even keel whereas all the others are slackers, lazy bums just sitting on their haunches."

Then soon the body stops cooperating and we eyes closing around us. Is this all? What was all this for?

The first reaction of humans to any general truth that would help us become more aware is of denial. Rather proving that there is much truth in the statement that makes people make the effort to deny it in whatever capacity possible.

To me this the perfect proof of the deep denial that we live in and which is impeding our growth into more Divine Beings.

All generalisations are collective thoughts which means of course there will be some exceptions that prove the rule. The elements that make up the human nature in different people are not different; composition of percentages differ. When we talk in general, we talk of the most prevalent elements.

When we talk of exceptions, it normally means that there is a wish to contradict or show off that we too know.

Different geographical areas and cultures develop a general character. In India the prevalent attitude is to let others be. We do not have the killing instinct and that is why we let others win - or in other words we let ourselves be beaten and overwhelmed placidly.

In India I have seen we are extremely sensitive to being poked and therefore we also take great care that we do not offend anyone as the demon of a hurt ego will come and stand in front and block everything. So we never come to the point, never aim our arrows to the heart, never answer precisely. We are just not sharp or curt enough and we dilly dally. At the same time we talk at length so that we are not misunderstood. This makes it easy for others to win over us and take advantage of us and manipulate us through reverse psychology mainly.

At the same time some of us who are more unscrupulous, we are aware of this tendency and use it to the full in personal relations to get what we want by using the weakness of the others against themselves.

This is why our bureaucracy is so corrupt because the public itself is too and the bureaucrats are no one else but us. To stop the corrupt practices, the masters make rules and safeguards which in effect only add to the corruption.

We are on the other hand experts at creating illusions. We are very good but that is the problem. We are somehow not geared to be the best.

We can be very cruel and very generous at the same time. I wonder if we have any idea of what and who we are. We are very like the sweet tangy and hot & sour mixture (food) that we like so much.

When we talk of humanity some words will catch our attention more than others; we should not personalise the philosophy but consider it and meditate on how deeply it has touched us one way or other.

But if I may say so from a deep occult point of view, our flexibility is just an illusion.

We can say that an opening and widening of the mind has begun since the last 200 or so years. This is something to be thankful for. But the journey has just begun and we cannot start thinking that all is well because we have only started exercising now the power the mind has and we are making quite an interesting mess over and about it.

Technically though we are like a fish in a bowl who is once at the south end and later at the north end.

On arguments: If we were two people with more open and flexible minds, then we would not be arguing would be?

Arguments happen when one is trying to prove the other wrong and insists to be heard; submission from the other is also expected.

The tendency of bringing everything down to the common lowest level is hurting progress in human evolution.

In the guise of being kind, humanity has junked "effort and expression" by talking of rights and deciding to wallow in the quagmire that they are. When you talk of raising standards, they talk of not interfering and letting people be or find their own way. Weak characters will unleash their cruel and violent side while the stronger ones will show kindness and compassion. The violent ones for now are having the upper hand.

On the other hand the simple concept s of doing "good" sometimes takes farcical forms and end-up as very cruel instances. When a minimum wage was guaranteed and made law, most people stopped employing expensive servants. Result was that the poor people, without any special abilities were denied the little that was coming their way. Machines to save labour were invented and the jobs became even scarcer. And the so called "creative" rich ones ended up doing everything by themselves. The devices instead of time saving started taking all our time.
The fight against child labour has become a farce and created more hungry children that are sold into more nefarious activities. It is a sad reflection that in my childhood, I could go 20 miles in any direction on my bicycle without fear but today I am so afraid of the world that I dare not leave my child out of my sight for a minute.

The human concept of kindness always somehow turns into a curse as it depends mostly by weakening the human spirit. Take again the assistance and support monetarily given to the jobless...has it helped? People are living off it and not ever trying to better their lives. I have met many foreigners living in India on this money as the amount they receive goes a long way here. The other result is that that they manage to survive on cheap junk food and now we have a huge sick population requiring heavy medical support. I don't remember ever seeing my grandmother sick.

Take for instance education. It is thought that education would bring better prospects. It has only made people into dreamers looking for white collar jobs while the farms beg for help to pick the fruits and vegetables. We have ended up creating a population of literates with some sort of diplomas in hand with some smattering of information which they do not know how to apply so in effect this education acquired over the entire growth period of the mind goes waste. Once the formative years are lost, there is little that can be done and for that matter anyone wants to do. The government is held liable to uphold their promises and the entire mass of people is out on the streets making life difficult for everyone.

The Fallacy of teaching -

1) That everyone can be taught

2) That everyone wants to be taught

3) Book learning is "learning".

4) A diploma is the thing to aim for.

Can you pour water in a tumbler when you don't even have one?

This is what it is when we forcefully set out to DISCUSS, Parley, TEACH to people who have not made available their minds.

They are what they are; take it or leave it.

Corrollary: Forced sending of children to schools is a waste of energy. Not letting them learn a trade naturally by acting as helper to their skilled parent is a crime. Saving the children from child labour is keeping them away from acquiring serious earning abilities.

Everyone understands that the world runs on the concept of "WHAT's IN IT FOR ME?". It is barter. You do something for me and I do something for you. Now the question is what can you do for me?

A great lot depends on what input has gone into forming the child. In the Ashram I had known only kindness, positive reinforcement and everyone taking care of each other like a huge family. Adults never scolded us, rather it was the opposite; the adults would listen to us seriously when we would often vent out our anger. All consciously trying to live to a higher level of consciousness.

But life has its twist and turns.

Suddenly I was thrown into the general world of "family" with all its intricate pushes and pulls love and enmities. I was floored.

It took me quite some years to learn to stand on my feet and I was astounded in contrast at the unnecessary violence being exercised in human relationships. Being right has always been the first goal of human existence; being superior and in control the second.

Most humans don't see this contrast as they have never seen the other side.

In conclusion my mind is set on the points that until the children are brought up right, this cannot change.

Today again there is this news of protecting women against violence.

We can easily go back at least 3 to 5000 years back with recorded writings and pronouncements all over the world with philosophers, saints, poets explaining the Nature of things and most importantly HUMAN NATURE.

Yet in our behavior and resultant resolutions of our mutual violence there is no difference or change or let up. I do end up asking why? And I have been asking this from day one because I have been at the receiving end since the last I can remember.

I have never blamed anyone but I always go back to the question, is it in me, or is it something from without or is it destiny or this is how life IS and will continue to be until some elementary basic changes are made in the Earth's consciousness???

I have lived through one mother, 3 aunts, sisters, cousins, 6 lady friends, guardians in hostels, teachers, 3 women bosses and workers, friends, associates of all hues alongside men of all hues too in every kind of situations in greater numbers in position of father, bosses, teachers and business associates, service providers and some friends.

In all this I realized one thing specifically. Anger develops where the mental maturity of an educated, well-travelled & widely experienced "MIND" is lacking.

I am often seething with anger but I control my thoughts and emotional responses and use my knowledge of human nature to manipulate rather than let loose my quarrelsome side which with my acting ability, control on words and understanding of reverse psychology can be rather daunting.

I have realized that I cannot reach these minds. The minds are set. The motions and notions are set. The subconscious is in absolute control and repeats itself.

If I try to reach them with words, nothing will happen. It is back to square one when we meet next. Advice, orders all go down the drain; even when medically important. Nothing registers. No effort to change or understand is made. If insisted too much you get back "argumentative backlashes".

It is frustrating, exasperating and that is how it is.

You can only back off if you can afford it.

The truth is emotional dependency makes us want to be together and mental disconnect separates us like a huge stone wall. Humans need to find a solution to this.

One of the ways that things could change is if children are taught about it from the beginning so that they understand in what kind of waters they will be swimming in life.

This little message by my Senior-most Teacher, The Mother of the Sri Aurobindo Ashram of Pondicherry makes clear:

Sweet Mother,

What is the best relationship between two human beings? Mother and son? Brother, friend or lover, etc?

All the relationships are good in principle and each one expresses a mode of the Eternal. But each can be perverted and become bad due to the selfish falsehood of human nature which prevents the vibrations of love from manifesting in their purity.
-The Mother

Where does Cruelty come from?

A lot of people misunderstand deliberately.

Why?

Because the opposite would require EFFORT. They have to first pay attention. Attention spans require energy. All their energies are focused on "NOT DOING"; what they call enjoying life which actually if seen properly is nothing but chasing pleasurable sensations like scratching an itch.

Then all listening requires follow-up. Means further energy has to be put in first to get off the bums and actually show that you mean what you are saying or agreeing to.

Complaining is preferred to solutions.

Another point is that when you misunderstand a new avenue opens for showing to others who is better and the boss. Humans are (I don't expect anyone to agree) sadistically inclined. In simple language it means that arguments, quarrels actually give us pleasure and an excuse to show-off.

Not intelligence but VANITY rules this world. If it does not agree with what I want it is wrong.!!!

This conversation I had and it shows rather lucidly our attitude to change and our attitude to listen to those who speak about it. The conversation exposes how we find arguments to avoid the issue.

Pradeep Pk Maheshwari

You missed this sentence: They rarely see the need for enlarging their view

Lady S: Rarely means sometimes, and some people try. Not many I admit, but we have high standards,PK!

Pradeep Pk Maheshwari: Are you taking it personally?

You must have noticed that I speak from the universal angle only or recount my personal stories. Nothing is ever intended towards anyone specifically.

All pondering about yourself is your own subconscious relating and it is all your connect with yourself and your duty to manage how you redecorate your home to suit yourself.

Lady S: I don't take things personally, but you can only comment from your point of view. How can you comment for 7,000,000.000 people in the world

Pradeep Pk Maheshwari:

At the base, universal level, the cosmos is from where we all come and there, at the roots everything is the same. The outer manifestation of course differs in permutations and combinations like all houses have salons, bedrooms, kitchens and bathrooms at the universal level but none is the same.

The olds sages who gave us the Occult insight into human affairs indicated this Indian division of the Cosmos into Devas and Rakshasa (demons).

The Devas are of course the ones who want to uplift and progress and ethically raise mankind into godhead. The purpose of the Rakshasa is to block this at every possible move; from the moral view-point this is utterly saddening and rather cruel and we can wonder exactly to what purpose?

In fact occult sciences say that the rakshasas are there to concretize our aspirations, intentions and efforts. They are a forging force. There is no easy way out. Either you will it and change like the yogis do or you get pushed in the crusher and are pulverized and recreated into a beautiful new you.

All these devastations that we see in life, all these blocks and tragedies are comparable to the tilling of the land for newer growth. If we listen to the Earth on moral principles, she would be saying that this tilling is hurting her and we should not be doing it. Is it not cruel to poke a long hard stick into her innards?

This attitude and behaviour shows not only in governance but also in the most intimate relationships. 9 out of 10 people I have met do not listen at all. They put a lot of energy in no listening. They react to certain words and are either off to blare out their often repeated short tapes running in their heads as recorded messages OR they simply lose interest attention and walk off or as most people today do, start paying attention to their phone. This is why narcissism is so widespread and even considered normal while humankind goes forward protecting their Cruelty induced Rakshasa nature with great cleverness. It is so much easier to learn to live with violence than to rise above it.

If you study all our developments, all our clichés and all the sermons, they all are hiding our basic natures so that the rakshasa nature does not show but we know it is there.

I notice that since the last 150 years the Rakshasa have been using the newly awakened mind of the humans to give us new products to amuse ourselves with and create great, more violent and gorier tragedies. That these thoughts, ideas and developments are indeed gifts from another world, fed into human minds that are ready to give them material form is a concept that western minds may find weird. We in the orient do not think of ourselves as the doer and thinker. Whatever, you will have to agree that it has become easier to commit crimes, bigger and better, with all these new technologies now at our disposal like cars, phones, digital automation and indestructible raw materials to give shape to new gadgets that allow us to live more perversely.

What is the silver lining? These are preparing us for eventual waking up. How long will this humanity suffer? No way to predict but the chain has to break someday. A few million years in the Earth's consciousness is really a short episode so don't even try to visualize or understand.

PS: One thing that needs to be understood about Rakhshas nature. They cannot see themselves as rakhshas and they do not see that their actions are going to hurt them for all their cleverness. There is an automatic process there that eventually completes the circle and destroys the perpetrator.

I have seen deeply into myself and anger and the urge to avenge is there. It comes over me now and then. When young I destroyed myself because of it and lost opportunities by the bucketful. But as my mind in its natural state lives in the domain of intelligence where it has seen that this activity only brings more pain I have learn to desist and look immediately away as fast as I can make myself to do so.

In my anger I have hurt people and I have seen how karma comes back waving its chains and floor me. Now I am more scared of the retribution and control my anger. I have also taught myself to forget. By keeping my peace I see more deeply into human nature and its convoluted ways; I have become more intuitive and can connect the chain of events that will ensue. The images of the results frighten me.

I have seen clearly that I am the perpetrator of my own violence. Somewhere it all begins in me.The others are all retaliating.

The mass of humans do not see where it begins. It is ever so clearly the fault of others. By this logic they absolve themselves. In this world neutral positions are not allowed. Do you remember how Ben Hur is confronted by his old bosom friend with "Either you are with me or you are not; if you are not then you are the enemy" and Ben Hur becomes the mortal enemy of the Roman general who was his closest friend. The pain and violence that ensues is beyond senseless. It is one sided but it cannot be stopped. Ben Hur does not respond back but he does protect himself and the result is that the Roman friend comes under his own chariot.

There is a spiritual issue here. We have to learn to not be allowed to respond to our impulses and see the consequences we bring upon ourselves. But the winning moments can be so sweet.

The mass of humans cannot be shown because their eyes are turned. The going issue here is that simply telling makes no impression. It has to be pounded into them if at all. Mother Nature has designed life with disasters and emotions for warfare. We cannot hurt back Mother Nature

After all what can you do against a storm?) so we sit back and weep but against others humans we let loose our martial tendencies. Especially when we know that the other person is not in a position to retaliate; then all our sadistic propensities gush out forth in all their blatant coarseness.

I have only one prayer: O Lord don't let me fall into the hands of these scoundrels who love hurting, are legally in a position to hurt and their sadistic tendencies.

Tell me Malachy, how many do you think adopt this way of thinking?

Malachy Matthews to Pradeep Pk Maheshwari,

And you know there are those who take the moral high ground and tut tut and their solution for this situation would be to cut the perpetrator's head off or send him to solitary confinement for 20 years; a similarly brutal act. The deep irony of it all.

The Mother of Pondicherry, Sri Aurobindo Ashram was talking of marriage for men and she said men shall never get out of their pettiness until they get out of the need for those small comforts of married life.

We are prepared to live in bondage, pay for it through our nose for the few moments that we deem important and we do not see life going farther than that.

The same attitude magnifies itself into our whole life as well.

Security and fear of what is coming keeps us thinking small.

Additionally we are prepared to fight, for these small comforts. We can become very cruel when our path is crossed.

Show them what is right.

Why is it that some people are so offended at just about everything; specially things that do not concern them, do not bite them and are otherwise naturally none of anyone's business?

For instance we can take the case of uproar by the white cultures and their opposition to breast feeding children first medically some 30-50 years ago and now in open places? While they want to see breasts everywhere in their lives like in journals, their dressing and even in adverts selling refrigerators. They talk of dressing up but focus on the undressing!

Has anyone thought of what is good for the baby? Why is this cruelty being imposed on the child?

What piques them?

After studying this a little even perfunctorily I realised that people who are offended are really weak character ones who find certain pictures and activities as attacks on their "weaknesses" - a kind of fear that they may expose themselves. Example: Take the Muslim men, they are so singularly sexual minded that they need to keep their women in burquas as otherwise they are always excited and can go berserk easily. The big news is that this vibration, in India too got passed on to the Hindus. And if one looks closely in history this factor raises its head every now and then in every culture when conservatives are in governance.

And to keep their charade of superiority they then can live only when the whole world follows their way.

A big way to maintain "divides" in society is by creating "Finger-raising" factors. This allows open and "fair" criticisms and the critics can pat themselves for the good deeds they are doing for society and its decadent ways.

Although it goes unsaid, but factors open to criticism also open doors for justified violence. Anything that can be termed immoral can then also be openly attacked and women are such lovely targets.

The Change has to be from Within.
What I have to say is not weak spirits or soft hearts.

Do you feel that if you show an attitude of Kindness and Compassionate Behaviour the Cruelty will stop?

Remember the cruel element is foraging for food it can devour. It is this stupid thinking of "Being Kind" that is their main dish.

Why? Because the kindness is NOT established in our hearts as a "BEING" – as an entity; in the present moment and condition it is a THOUGHT" based on certain protocols that we have established in our minds as being kind and unkind. The actions that sprout out of this thinking are also protocol behavior which do not really stem from the core of our being. This makes them a charade to enjoy for the moment; nothing else. Nobody is fooled; least of all our selves but we all as a group and civilization maintain a common smiling front which is a totally dishonest image like on the silver screen.

To Think

What I understand from this word is: Real thinking. Where you sit down quietly. Reflect. Ponder. Let your subconscious provide data. Ruminate. Then when all the other factors like personal emotions, prejudices have been all well considered and the pros and cons studied - a decision is taken and

sometimes not at all.
 Cruelty couldn't exist under these conditions.

"What is the hardest task in the world? To think.: Ralph Waldo Emerson"

Is it surprising then, at the core, the world is not changing and every weakness of human nature is exploited ever more. The devil has no kindness. It has a single voracious character. It feeds on weakness and grows. You cannot influence it by small gestures and good wishes because its responses are as temporary as your behavior pattern.

The human persona is 99% subconscious which is a doorway to many entities and forces that have had opportunities to be established and use us as instruments. That is where the change is required. We should become "KINDNESS" so that the other forces cannot find a doorway to enter our consciousness and influence our behavior. Certain actions, Activities, Feelings and Responses should become impossible thru our persona.

How will you know where you are in your personal spiritual emancipation? The world will throw you in some cauldron and then you can see for yourself the responses that come out forth from you.

Cruelty in Love.

We seem to be unleashing more violence in the name of Love than war. This is life on earth with humans. When we purportedly love something or someone the word "possession" as in the phrase POSSESSION IS Nine Points of the Law is more in evidence than Affection or Kindness.

The need to possess and obtain our object of desire seems to take over our spirit and for this purpose with this as our goal we go after it with all the vigour that we can muster. You have only to look closely and you will see how violent and untruthful our wooing can be and is. Infatuation is a better word. We impose ourselves almost like a blanket on the other person or object with a gun in hand to make our point clear that once we have decided to OWN the object of desire, nothing will thwart us.

I am thinking of the recent story that I saw in the media. A young lady near Delhi became the Love object of one of the nouveau rich young men (LOUTs of the modern era) of the area. He started wooing her which was in fact "Stalking" of the worst kind with physical intimidation. He even proposed. She would have none of it. In the feudal minded, man-dominated psyche of India this is seen as an insult. So the man tried to kidnap her. This failed so he shot her in the head. He, as he told the police later, was certain that she could be happy only with him.

Ownership seems to be the greater factor in human love. We appreciate something. We want it and not just want it but also own in and have it within the borders of our worldly property. We really do not pay attention but this is the story of humans from the last we can remember. The most famous story is of Helen of Troy. Would you call this a Tragedy or a Love story or a War story? The nonsensical gory 10 year epic that unfolded is a pain. Something similar is seen in the story of Mahabharata that is narrated in India.

When I look at all this clinically I am astounded as my experience is that it is familiarity and nearness that creates the emotion of love and confidence to develop and mature between people. In this scenario the face and museums standard beauty means nothing. All women are basically beautiful when they appreciate you and show it in their eyes.
As for wanting a female body to play with, any female should normally do or one can go to a courtesan.

But to insist that you must have the woman who has your attention can mean only one thing and that is that you are making it a matter of prestige - No love here.

Today in modern life things are really no different. In the guise of love our concern and attachment seems to project itself out as DOMINANCE - the arrogance and possession are more in play. There is very little love there. All love stories are exceptions and point hopefully to a better humanity but not just yet.

The saying Familiarity breeds contempt should not be forgotten. Contempt when backed by power of position or money can bring the ogre out from within us and this is now happening more often than not. In this material world, materially speaking, there is so much to be arrogant about now in this 21st century!

Rape + filming + putting it on internet

The sense of power this kind of activity gives has gone asunder. It is kind of a banner advert announcing "See my power - and no one can touch me"

It has always been there in the human make-up.

But digital video that can go all over the world in seconds has simply brought terror into every hand/home.

Humans watch videos and clips to find out if it is good or bad or worth watching or not. Abominable and stupid and CRUEL: this is what this world is surfacing as; something that it always was but its spread was limited by lack of travelling ability and means.

Do you all, anyone thinks that this is the best way to expose humans and force them to accept how vile they really are and then subsequent change will perhaps follow?

Malachy Matthews

I think there is kindness in most humans. I think organisations corrupt human kindness.

Pradeep Pk Maheshwari

Kindness gets coated over by greed, the need to possess and collect/store for further use. It is a reflection of how our minds work on any given subject.

The mind is a collector. In the name of knowledge we collect books. In the name of being loved, we collect friends, in the guise of being seen important we collect cars, paintings and crystal "objet d'art".

The only kind person is a child who has no need to worry about where things are coming from. He can afford to be kind, giving and loving. Human adults are kind to each other only when it helps mask their own faults.

My daughter when she was just 8 took all the money she found in the house which ran in thousands to her school and distributed it to her class mates so that they could buy books at the exhibition being held there by a bookseller. Luckily for us we found this out early and the director of the school helped us retrieve the money.

All the books were returned to the book-seller who kept quiet about it all although as protocol demanded she should have informed the director of the school that something was amiss as he was following his dharma of selling books and it was not his business to ask where these 8 year olds were getting all these thousands of rupees.

We are part of the crowd. We did our part. Now we have to wait and watch.

I neither speak for myself nor you.

I have already explained that I speak of the Universal mind and how it is being used in this world by humanity in general.

One of the aspects is that people cannot understand or relate to any writings , words outside of their relationship to themselves.

They personalise it and act and react accordingly. Mostly it ends up as misunderstandings. Often it creates heated arguments and quite often it is the reason for the start of disenchantment or quarrel.

A story from a friend who does not want to be named.

As I said, I feel that the greatest cruelty can present itself in the clothes of kindness. I worked for many years for a large multinational company here in Ireland. When I look back at what happened I realise that what happened to me was due to my own weakness and arrogance. I under-performed in my management role as I believed I was undervalued by the organisation. Perhaps now, looking back, it was because I over-valued myself. I had reason to do so because my academic achievements were far superior to those of my colleagues. But I tended to consider myself superior to everyone anyway. I was a 'snob' perhaps. On the other hand I always treated people with respect, I think.

Looking back, I was a child, I think.

The department in which I worked seemed to run itself and I never really put much effort into improving performance as a Manager. I remember someone said to me once that I was more of a Janitor' than a manager. The comment hurt me, but I laughed obviously as I was intellectually superior and more academically qualified and earned triple the salary of the person who made the comment. I had worked in the same role for about 7 years in a management role and the company was lazy and lackadaisical. The company was then taken over and became extremely frenetic and competitive.

At some stage, an element in management decided they wanted me out of the role while a certain few others recognised my potential compared to that of my peers. I could pull people's logic apart at meetings and inspire silence. I became hated by my peers and by many others. My direct manager challenged me on many occasions, passively and aggressively. In the end I was 'demoted' -not formally; just given a less important role and my salary and benefits were the same. The prime mover was a female colleague who resented my lack of work. She was also having an affair with my boss.

We used to have department nights out and soon after the "demotion", on one such occasion; I was approached at such an event by two colleagues at a slightly superior level who slapped me on the back and said "Aaaw we heard what happened to you; that was so unfair". "You don't have to put up with this". And with tremendous sincerity one of them suggested that I "jump off the train"; leave the company. Of course I replied that was out of the question as I had a mortgage to pay at the time. There was a lot of alcohol consumed that night; typical Irish pub night out. I just remember their behaviour because I am not a political person and I take everything that someone says at face value.

But I am sure in retrospect that they were set up that night to convince me to leave the company. The "prime mover" I refer to who had the affair with my direct boss was not there but it so happened she was also the "official" partner of one of the people who spoke to me. Yes' it's always complicated! It was their fake sympathy that really got to me and the exhortation to "jump off the train".

Again, in my naivety I did not see the truth of the movement within my department to get me to leave the company. Of course there is a lot more context and background to this story.

The most cruel person, in my opinion was my direct boss who was orchestrating this maneuver. Had he sat me down and said "Look you are in trouble, but let me help you"; "Do A, B and C, I could have recovered from the situation". But he was a 'Manager' by name only; he hadn't a clue. He failed me. He should have slapped my face and supported me but instead allowed me to suffer many years of misery because of my incompetence and his incompetence.

It is the sweet, dirty, dishonest rhetoric that people use that is at the center of this memory of cruelty for me. I had huge strengths (as proven later) and huge weakness in attitude which could have been corrected with some guidance. I was young and naïve with huge potential. I needed a different kind of 'cruelty'. A slap in the face. If someone had just held my hand for a while, I could have let go and walked to the stars.

PK:
This story reminds of an episode with my father. My father belonged to a huge industrial group of India and was in it due to family connections of old. He was in it as a valued member because of the paternal connections. But as things happen, the old man of the group died, the sons took over, the company was broken up and new family members of the original owner came in etc. my father was managing their lime-stone quarries and my father recommended a friend of his for Technical Manager in the group as this friend needed a job. Within a year this fiend convinced the

owner that all the problems were due to the lack of managerial ability of my father. My father was asked to leave after 40 years of devoted service and being treated as a child of the family. Luckily another branch of the family immediately called him and put him on another better project but the shock and adjustment to new people was great. His philosophical attitude to life saved him from psychological disaster. I was there too. But the cruelty of the whole episode shook me and was an eye-opener on the fickleness of human considerations.

All said and done our relationships are based on immediate self-interest and if we have to be cruel about it: SO BE IT.

India is very behind in PRE-EMPTIVE thinking. What I understand from this word is: Real thinking. Where you sit down quietly. Reflect. Ponder. Let your subconscious provide data. Ruminate. Then when all the other factors like personal emotions, prejudices have been all well considered and the pros and cons studied - a decision is taken and sometimes not at all.

This is the reason it is never prepared. It is unbelievable how philosophical we are and how IMPRACTICAL. Pragmatism in Indian culture is at its peak. We wait and do nothing till the moment is upon us. Why waste any time in agonizing.

We believe deeply in crossing the bridge when it comes,
Living in the moment to the point that I would call ourselves
CRUEL.

We have this sarcastic saying "They will go to dig the well
when the fire has started"

Take these scenarios. There is a fork in the road. But you
take the short cut on the left. 10 kms ahead you come
across a barrier saying road closed due to repairs. You ask
yourself why this board could not have been put 10 kms
earlier at the fork. Indians don't think that far. The signage
of road is closed can be put only where it is closed isn't it? A
little detour….how does it matter? Think of it as adventure;
it will teach you to take life with pinch of salt.

We want to fulfill our commitments with the least effort
and with the shortest cuts possible. Cleverness and cunning
has taken this far in the last 300 years and there seems to
be no good reason to become more vigilant, more futuristic
and "KINDER" and make life easier for others. No! We pride
ourselves in our ability to get away with it with our cruel
dispositions. The sense of power this gives us is so
exhilarating.

This amounts to cruelty in my thinking by the in-charges of
public interest but their salary is confirmed by the
government treasury and who cares for the public?! It is as I

see it, sadistic subconscious at work. I have always
wondered how it came to be so.

In India I notice that when we try to communicate with
another the other person listens to you only when what you
say tallies exactly with what he is thinking or wants or has
already decided what is acceptable. Otherwise the sound is
muted off. You simply do not get to him. Arguments and
sometimes leading to violent ones are the only result if you
insist or think you can drum something into them. You
finally end up accepting that you don't matter, no one really
matters, and nothing really matters. It is a cruel scenario but
this is the reality and we glorify in it.

Human nature as seen on earth just yet is rather
quarrelsome. It has great need to justify itself and the
violence is bubbling under the surface at all times. Our
intellectual process is its ally. So we always have in any
society wherever that it may be..... Certain values that have
been decided by common consent are given the aura of
superiority or commonality. These values then are imposed
by common consent over the group and all those not
accepting or not having these values become alien to the
group or inferiors.

This gives us the excuse to perpetuate violent crimes and
justify cruelty with glee. When you think of cruelty, think of
Honor Killings in families, Sati and the Inquisition and
Hitler's horror that was inflicted on the people of this earth.
Just imagine the suffering of tying of feet in China, The
entire slave trade which continues to this day as bonded

labor and controlled imprisonment of street workers in the flesh trade. The unbelievable pain inflicted on stolen children that is only increasing. We have to only note the burning of brides in India and the throwing out of widows to fend for themselves in this cruel world at the mercy of "men" looking for satisfaction even if the objects of their desire were to be destroyed – something that is worse than murder.

In every culture and every moment in history humans have shown how manipulative and degenerate they can be. This seems to be the main trait of the human race for now.

One really needs to ask why Kindness did not take root in human consciousness. Why the human race takes pleasure in instilling fear, depression, disgust and despair in whoever they touch.

Malachy Matthews

Malintent clothed as kindness is the worst cruelty.

I'll tell you a story that comes to mind and you know it was only years later that the true meaning of what happened dawned on me. This is the case in many remembered traumatic events. This one doesn't relate to 'cruelty' per se but it insists on coming to mind. Many years ago I was working with a lady whose son was having awful difficulties at school through being bullied. He had been forced to leave two schools and was now facing the prospect of completing his Leaving Cert (Irish high school diplomat at 17yrs of age or so). I felt a deep sense of anger and injustice about this and this lady confided in me. The formal school system didn't seem to suit this young man at all and the prospect of entering a third school was nil as his confidence had been shattered. It seemed that a more informal setting with mature students - i.e. adults or those with some special needs etc. After a bit of research I discovered the perfect solution and confirmed this young man's eligibility to complete his course in an alternative way. I felt so proud of myself for achieving this and I handed details and phone numbers to my lady colleague who thanked me. She then gave me the silent treatment for about a week and refused to answer any questions about how things had developed with her son. I was completely puzzled but decided to let things be; I had spent a lot of time trying to help this young man whom i had never met. It struck me as quite an unjust reward from the mother. I forgot about the situation for years and, upon recalling it suddenly dawned on me that as far as this mother was concerned I had in some way usurped or undermined her role and she felt angry about it. I also have stories where someone who in the past was indifferent to me became very conscious of my welfare and who started giving me career advice. It was only a year later that I realised the full context and their true motives. Perhaps I am slow; I don't do politics and take people at face value. Naïve would be a better word perhaps.

Pradeep PK Maheshwari:
Malachy, in response to your story I would say she was looking for sympathy and not really a solution. I have heard of many stories where the mother wishes to be seen as "Long-suffering".

I remember reading about a mother in USA who was feeding water from the toilet to her son and keeping him perpetually sick. She would spend nonstop days and nights at the hospital at his bedside and became to be seen in the neighborhood as a saint. The doctors were totally perplexed and eventually zeroed it down to her.

In my case my mother had to do nothing as far taking care of me was concerned. A servant was assigned to me. The cook fed me. Father was taking care of the medical needs. She was disturbed for nothing. But she saw in my sickness a good avenue to complain and be seen as the long suffering mother. She even banned my brother and sister to talk to me as I was not a nice person.

What is "NICE"?

When a woman is chained and raped everyday it is just a misdemeanor but when she finds the opportunity to kill her tormentor it is not nice and it becomes "murder" the worst crime.

When a boss torments his employee it is nothing but if the employee raise his/her voice it is not nice and the employee can be thrown out.

The teacher can cane the child but if the child protests it is not nice and if the parents speak up the child is removed from school.

The man can enjoy an extramarital affair but if the woman is found out it is not nice and she is stoned to death.

Humans have such Nice ways to hide their cruelties. When we judge do we take into account the narrative? No; because we have labeled some activities as nice and others not and we follow protocol in judgment - without thinking or studying the cases.

Do you see the undercurrent of cruelty in this behaviour pattern?

The not so transparent cruelty of our thinking and resolves.

All cruelty is not visible or always initiated with ill-will. But yet we do end up inflicting a lot of hurt which finally does come back in a cyclic way to haunt and hurt us too. Doctors make mistakes. Generals give bad orders. Parents do things to the child under the pressures or understanding or knowledge of the moment in time. Even the well-wished good often ends up creatively cruel.

What I have come to see is that most of the cruel moments sprout from all activities having selfish motives as seeds where the "I" comes first regardless of the pain and ill feelings that are created all around; as long as the end result is what we had desired. The future has no eyes to see they say. The present is all we have got say the philosophers and the people literally live it this way.

Let me give you two stories from life that prove that not all good advice is given with good intentions and that the bad always does not result in disaster.

I was in the Ashram and reluctant to come out of the magical atmosphere and life I was leading there. My first question is why I was singled out for the experience that followed. I could have stayed in the Ashram and followed my Soul's path as others of my classmates did and are still there. But no I was singled out for something more it seems. My parents would visit me once a year. In one visit my mother took me to a lonely spot in the garden and spoke seriously to me about my eating habits. This is where my journey really began.

(In retrospect one can see how the ground was being laid for my development and how the Divine used it to shape me up).

She talked to me about the excessive appetite I had. According to her I would become sick, end up having a huge belly that would burst. She made it clear that I need to eat less and I was so frightened by the scenario that this is exactly what I started doing. We were in those years very active and even though I was hungry most of the time surrounded by food in front of me in plenty I was too scared to eat my full. Soon a pain in the back developed and I did complain to our Ashram doctor who was well aware of my mischievous disposition and simply scoffed at me and shooed my out saying no-one at my age gets back-pain. When my parents came I told them too and they thought I was simply complaining because I was not serious about my studies. No one was listening to me! I was actually being faulted and derided for shamming.

This went on for another year and then when it became impossible, the elders finally took me seriously and I was checked up medically. Nothing serious was found but it was decided to pull me out and be taken home. There my case was again checked by the local senior surgeon of the important hospital and X-rays etc. were sent to my doctor uncle because the pain was excruciating and would not go away. Finally after a whole year it was found that my spine had carries – a kind of TB infection that results from malnutrition and general debility. I was just fourteen and had already lost 2 years of my life in pain and deprivation.

Now started a life of doctors and more regular checkups and finally it was decided to put me in a plaster of Paris jacket and as this was 1962, the advent of antibiotics had caught the imagination, the new, very promising drug Streptomycin was used to treat me. It was so new that I was over-dosed by double but the doctors did not know it then.

Six months in the Plaster of Paris jacket was an experience that has now made claustrophobic and whenever I am stressed I just want to be in the open in nature and then it was removed but I was made to wear a splint. The X ray showed that the hole in the spine was filling up and my father in his wisdom decided now that I was on the way to recovery I could stop all medication and worrying about it. The pain soon returned and when we went back to the surgeon he said that the disease had relapsed. By now I had lost 3 years under the feudal thinking of my parents and my mother was not ready to put up with a sick child, argumentative and demanding to boot on her hands any more. I was unwanted and my faults were too many and I tended to argue and think for myself.

So I got termed as the rotten apple and was continuously even abused for it. But this is what alienated me from the entire huge family and I had to find my own new way. This took me into an Arabian Nights kind of life that gave me everything I wanted that I would never got had I stayed cocooned in my family's arms.

I used to visit my parents once a month for a weekend. My sister was with them. One morning I started talking of sister's marriage as was the next step in her life and of course it would be an arranged one. My point was that the men are influenced greatly by what they "see" and therefore it would be wise to not let her figure spoil and keep it in good trim etc. My mother did not like what I was saying because it showed her as failing her daughter. Her pride was sorely hurt and an argument began which it always did whenever I spoke at home. My father was sitting by and he lost his temper and asked me point blank that if I did not like the way things were run in the house I should go back to Delhi to my own place and stay there.

That is the day when the penny dropped. I decided to take the harsh cruel road and lay the grounds for further clear-cut relationship. If my father and elders in my family felt that they could be judgmental and punish me as and when it pleased them, I would clearly show them that this was not acceptable. I did the unthinkable. I knew it would hurt but then if this was the only way then this surgical was a necessity as to me this attitude towards me needed to stop right there. And I got back at my father saying - "This is my house. I was born here. If you don't like it you are welcome to spend your time in your office whenever I am here"... he was so shocked at this belligerent insubordination that he shut up and we were good friends after that for life. He was basically a kind man but his behavior was so influenced totally by the feudal structure of our lives in India. I have seen parents/husbands who 9 out of 10 times throw the child/woman out and think later. How can anyone get that cruel?

A depressed person is adding to the difficult times all others are going through too. This is insidious cruelty.

From the occult angle there is a Force in the Universe which we call the Vital. It is a kind of life force. It is in all of us and at the primary level it is vane and narcissistic.

But this side of its character can be molded into becoming kind and generous and strengthened by educating the mind and reason by given examples, experiences and training right from the day of birth or even earlier (remember the art of war learnt by Arjun's son in the womb).

Once the child reaches 16 or so the vanity part becomes pronounced and after that it is difficult to coach or change its ways.

We go thru life "wanting this and desiring that". That is an ego habit of sorts.

When we don't get it we tend to be depressed and when we lose it we are terribly despondent. Strong minds soon get over it and learn to live with it with eyes on the future.

Weak minds pine over it and live in the past and often use it as a tool to gain sympathy which is basically again selfishness.

Quarreling Religionists: The mental level of both sides is the same.

IS IT NOT obvious (farcially speaking) that the world has become a better place because Ram. Krishna, Buddha, Jesus and Mohammed passed thru here?

Ignorant minions; looking for meaning in a goal-less life.

Self-proclaimed wise-men showing the way to others and correcting the faults that they have decided that humanity is following. The only loser is God.... whatever, whoever this Being is.

This is the way men create drama and self-importance for themselves.

This world is an amusement park. Just sit in your rocking chair and enjoy the show.

The sadness is in the part that the episodes are repetitive and predictable.

My focus is mainly on laws trying to govern human behaviour like in control of alcohol consumption, drugs, prostitution, suicide and such. Has it helped any? All laws based on imposing moral controls re worthless and should go.

Yes - it has helped cirminalise society.

Example: the drug trade. The peddler is afraid. The corrupt police are into a profitable protection racket. Once you are in you cannot leave this trade alive as you become a danger to others in it. So you get killed for sure when you are merely suspected. The victims are created assiduously by taking advantage of their weak spirits. It creates long term clients and a broken social structure that they feed upon even more. (It is another matter that the modern pharma and medicine has thinkers running the show with the same mentality but they have organised themselves to operate long term legally and give the image of saints trying to help us live better.)

Take for example prostitution. Women are shouting from roof-tops that it is their body and their decision but this is only as far as for abortion purposes. On what grounds is this activity illegal? It has only given the police and society to marginalise good women who have nowhere else to go and there is now a slave trade which suits all the governors beautifully.

Humans want to put up a great show of being "good and virtuous" but alcohol is not seen as a product that should be "controlled" like they control prostitution because for some reason society is not against it and it brings good revenue for the governors.

I say: Humans should not be stopped from making a mess of their lives if they so choose to.

It is part of the spiritual learning process. But for this we also need to first understand that life and rebirth, the continuity of the process of evolution etc is an ongoing process. Death does not end it and the concept of purgatory is essentially wrong.

PS: I do understand that the bad habits of some can be a danger to others. Let people decide what they will tolerate and give them the tools and permission to hit back without being afraid.

This "The law will take its course" philosophy has degenerated to a point where criminals are now more comfortable, living better, less afraid than the average Joe. Are we promoting cruel conditions on ourselves?

The governors can govern only when the people are too foolish to know better. Naiveté is built-in us so that we can as children look forward with fresh eyes. The adults, parents specially have always known this. They misuse this propensity to feed the child's mind and conscious to create replicas of themselves as extensions of their selves. There is no aim to make the children into something bigger and better and greater. So the parenting methods have always been to keep the child safe and uninformed or rather there was never any attempt to see beyond the childhood stage when we see the child as babies to be cared for.

Most grown up adults are actually at the mind level, still children. Very few people really cross the mental age of 14 in their lives.

It was so even in the Stone Age.

This psychological trait is so strongly ingrained and rooted in the human psyche that anyone with a modicum of intelligence and cleverness can fool the individual most of the time.
And we can be very cruel about it.

How to develop kindness?

Learn as much as you can about the world you are living in.
Read the news items and note how cruel we can be.
Broaden your knowledge base by reading history - not only of your own country but other countries too.

Learn how powerful Mother Nature is. Learn its secrets and all the healing sciences practiced in different areas of the world.

Learn about humans. Study psychology, anthropology and what different people, authors have to say and the stories they relate.

When you have broadened the mind this way, you will see a common streak flowing. You will see how common, inconsiderate and cruel we are. Our pride will become less prominent and our kindness will bloom. Our intelligence will open up and Universal wisdom will start flowing thru our minds.

It is something in the human psyche. I wonder how human it really is. Even at the individual level we show a kind of stubborn vindictive harshness that no one would ever believe if you told them. We hear stories of basic cruel behaviour everyday and we think of them as isolated news items and ignore them. We see it happening in our lives among our families yet we take them with a pinch of salt as part of life without ever thinking of them as calculated show of cruelty wherever we can get away with it.

Starving people for profit has been a continuous story in mankind's history. For some reason butchering whole populations seems to be fun.

At the present level of our civilisation note how people are filling up swimming pools for their luxury and to show off more than swim while the rest of the people go without it as the lakes go dry and disappear.

How hard hearted you must be to take all this water, bottle it and sell it.

People don't see the cruelty in this incongruous act all over the world? So we can safely conclude that humans invite it all upon themselves.

A lot of things we invite upon ourselves because of our legendary apathy, laziness and inertia (tamas) while trying to fulfill our desires.

The strong evil ones also seem to easily find followers and as an organized group they becomes a force that is in control and unstoppable. The first thing that comes to their minds is genocide and destruction. Why?

The gentle ones hide and live in fear.

Look at it from another angle. Communist thinking is really good.

It is a brilliant thought implant by the Forces whose job it is to make us conscious thru suffering if need be.

Considering the laziness aspect of the human consciousness this thought takes prominence that "WE ARE ALL EQUAL" because we have two arms and two legs and we all need to be judged by the physical work that we put in visibly so.

No intellectual activity allowed as that would show how unequal we really are. And like all the residents in a community or ashram or boarding house, the best way to keep the Peace is by all having the same level of dress, goods and poverty.

This cuts out all showing off, keeps the monkey mind occupied in "tiring" activities and the mind worried with where the next meal will come from.

By keeping the public from being exposed to the world, a kind of latent, tamasic peace is achieved.

No turmoil. No hankerings. Just go about having babies - an activity that requires no effort by the state to provide any infrastructure.

Hospitals and such? Come on... be real - they are better off dead anyway!

I am meeting so many women who have this creative energy to bring in change but they are so deeply engrossed with the "safety" factor that they have caged themselves in their ritualistic married lives and refuse to look beyond the walls of their garden. Their entire focus and energy goes in maintaining their equal status with their husband or "man".

How this has raised the CRUELTY quotient in this world is deliberately not recognized. I think it is actually foremost in the minds of all but not acknowledged by simply being ignored and pushed under the carpet as it does not serve the purpose of the male. It has been lost under the thought waves of Sin and Virtue that now hover on humanity like dark clouds.

Women too now see themselves simply as objects of desire with pride and have reduced their own vision of their selves as just "the female of the species". They ARE their boobs and all relationships begin and end with the vagina.

Can't people see how the bikini has become the focus of our culture and all that it purports to hide or in my view accentuate.

They is no more the Goddess Durga. The world wanted them as an "attraction" wherein their boobs and the shape of their legs alone mattered; and they obliged.

It is awful when ones sees how the attitudes have degenerated to women living and accentuating their boobs and protecting them from mishandling and making it the basis of all relationship with the world at large.

The separation of the persona is complete. We are no more people with hearts and minds and friendly brotherly/sisterly dispositions. We are now coins in the objectified world of material values and our values of importance are based cleanly on the monetary value our head carries.

The focus on the "female" is so high that a large swathe of the world lives only by it, focuses only on it and this has given rise to a cruel trade now enveloping the children that result from it and even outside of it. The women were fooled into believing the cruel lies of the wooing males who made them feel like princesses for a day and then imprison them for life into small airless cubicles. These were the lucky ones.

The unfortunate ones are forced to live "lives" that are worse than that of abandoned dogs on the street. How this is acceptable is beyond me? The lack of any tinge of affection and compassion that humanity shows is in my view not human at all. Just imagine a laborer in India giving birth to daughters because he can then sell them to traders in prostitution or as a bonded labour later. So if he has (let us say) even 3 daughters, his life is made. And the woman cooperating with him what would you say to that?

The amusing part is that the women fell for it and today one can see how they live in this false image. Half of this world's corruption stems from this attitude. (The other half is the greed for gold which can be easily satisfied by using women as tools).

Deeper research has shown that women are a strong link in this chain of spreading cruelty.

The priests may well stand in their pulpits and call it all wrong but they forget that they started it all by their labeling of human relations into either sinful or virtuous if they did not follow the male religion shopkeepers.

I see all the energy of these good people going towards maintaining the status quo which indirectly assists the negative forces to continue existing.

I wish to tell them that they are from the group of GIVERS. Nothing and nobody will ever be able to take anything away from them. But FEAR has them in control and nothing impresses them. Their minds are as yet not strong enough for it. Our need to be appreciated over-rides all considerations and we are suckers for appreciative gestures and we allow ourselves to be trapped in it.

Sadness is a component of Joy.

Sadness serves two functions. It helps to quieten down and contemplate. We pity ourselves sure as we are basically selfish but the mind also tends to replay and in the replay it sees its own role in the whole event too. The people with a sincere attitude see their error and build up on it to greater success. The insincere ones see the error of others and think of everything but the growth and/or improvement this event offers as an experience and lesson. Often the highly trauma-corrupted kind takes it as an attack on their persona and all their plans for the future becomes revenge scenarios.

Latest PK's quotes

They'll not want you to do anything that makes you independent of them. Pk

Beware of people who "THINK", act, react, respond, reply, decide & interfere based on what is convenient/comfortable to them. Pk

The honest in this corrupt world withdraw and keep withdrawing and eventually retire into ascetics. Pk

Why don't we like the truth coming from children and young people? Pk

Naiveté is built-in us so that we can as children look forward with fresh eyes. The adults, parents specially have always known this. They misuse this propensity to feed the child's mind and conscious to create replicas of themselves as extensions of their selves. pk

If I remember correctly, most of my life has gone waiting for something or the other. pk

Quarreling Religionists: The mental level of both sides is the same. Pk

As if it matters that you live or die. Look at the way they live their own lives - carelessly. Pk

Grief is the result of the Selfish pain we feel when we feel we have lost something which was an important emotional support. Pk

What can you do with people who get a high by un-nerving themselves? Pk

Yes; we are so focussed on the final destination that we forget to pay attention to the road leading there. Pk

Human minds prefer to go nitpicking on useless info and statistics as this permits them to argue, waste time in the guise of understanding but actually in the occult world it is well known that the mind is escaping engagement and not really wanting to learn. Pk

For a moment remove all your thoughts that stem from your learning from the Religion Library in your head? What is left? Pk

Don't use the word LEARNED. You have simply collected new data which sort of agrees to your pre-conceived better judgment. Pk

The phrase "in my opinion..." is one of the emptiest, devoid of meaning or sense - phrase. For the simple reason that one's opinion has really meaning only to the speaker and often I wonder if even this is true. Pk

Lord, make us capable to receive your unending rain of mercy. pk

Philosophy and Reflection.
I had entered life, fought my way in and got trapped & isolated by my own strength. I called Krishna and got trapped even further. There was only one way out and avoiding confrontation was not it. So I said "In for a penny; in for a pound" and jumped in the deep end and had to then by force learn to swim and get out of the pool. I can say Krishna helped like a good coach but relentless in pushing me on and always throwing me back into the pool.

This world can be extremely unforgiving - like deep waters if you don't know how to swim.

I literally learnt to swim and then float without effort.

Leaders we have but not leadership.

The people are not ready to go anywhere.

We just want to wallow where we are. - Effortlessly.

The thought that has sustained this mirage is "If it is written in our fate then nothing can stop it and if not then no effort will be fruitful".......sit back and enjoy.

India requires governance by leaders who understand the basic psychology of the human being from the occult/spiritual angle and practicalities of management of resources. Unfortunately those who have this capacity stay away from the crowds.

Politics is a mine-field of insincere, corrupt louts. Who in his right mind wants to be there?

Our personal philosophy is simple: Go and do whatever you want as long as you leave me alone - we have never understood the fact that no one is ever left alone - this is one of the hidden agendas governing our lives.

I am master of my life.
This is the stupidest way to look at life.

Destiny is the WAVE that put us where we are. What are you going to decide? What decisions have you been able to take since the day you were conceived? How much choice do you really have?

All we can say is that we shall decide what mess we create in all the little things that come to us and we do. Sure; our illusions make life easier to bear but we are only making it more complicatedly cruel for ourselves.

The rough, gruff and the vulgar pride themselves in their play with lower propensities of human nature. I suppose it is a kind of "dare" one puts up to society and the world in general.

It is equal to tying a stone to one's neck and jumping in the lake. But you realise this only when the sinking/drowning has begun and it is too late.

Don't think anyone is impressed or interested.

If it gets too boring, the world may have to lock you out too.

Kindness and compassion are the topics of this present moment on earth but humans learn soon enough that kindness is soon forgotten and often misconstrued as hurtful gestures. All those with a kind bend have also many experiences of rejection, being forgotten. Humanity in its arrogance can rarely accept that they were helped as gratitude has very little space in our lives. The ones who were helped easily rationalise that the helpers must have got something like some profit out if it all.

The unhappy ones use your gestures as a focal point to blame for all their pains.

After all good things that happen to us are deserved; the result of our virtuousness, gifts from the gods and the karmic cycle etc etc.

The mind cannot, will not, wants not to meditate because it is a perpetual machine. Will power can stop it backed by the Intuitive Domain that understands.

But to connect to the intuitive mental state one needs to quieten the endless spinning of the mind.

So how will this vicious cycle be stopped or broken?

Respond with controlled intent: To be successful.

Nothing in this life is more confusing than people who respond with intent.

We normally expect people to react in a particular pattern that is particular to each of us; something that we understand about each other after a few meetings. We then pattern our advances to suit the needs of the moment with calculated behavior from our side to make certain that the other person responds in a given manner as desired by us.

People are generally a cluster of habits, philosophy and they respond within an established frame-work that they call "ME". This is easily read and manipulated. Most of us are so enclosed in a habitual pattern that it is impossible to reach us on any other platform as we become closed entities and therefore predictable and immediately labeled as useless or useful and on the basis of this label kept away or made friends with. A lot of effort goes in these manipulations.

But the mind can be educated to rise above the instinctual and operate with controlled reason and the behavior patterns reigned in with will power and intent. People who learn to do this use all the information at their disposal and all the learning from their experiences to act, and respond. It is all a very controlled act. They are normally read all wrong and they are not predictable because they play life as a chess game. This is the secret of success in this world.

Project yourself with intent. We do this naturally only when we are wooing. It may be any kind of wooing; for attention by a partner, or a job, to get discounts or any such interest of very personal benefit. We need to rise a step or two higher and learn to think and "do". And as far as possible think well and act with kindness (but this is another subject for another time).

Compare the way James Bond responds to people and situations with the people in general. The intent and my words will become so totally clear.

James Bond should be seen as a yogi. A YOGI is someone who responds with intent. A YOGI is not the guy-in-the-street. He has mastered his reactions and responses or at least he is on the way to do so. It is difficult to gauge him for more often than not he deliberately gives out wrong signals to avoid people and situations of no interest to him.

The Play of Power and other Forces.

Trump has done what he was placed there to do by the Universe. He showed us our faults and shook the world. Now it is up to us to make a better world order. Let's see if we'll or let the old guard win

----

The "Evil" is the simplified Christian way of looking at it. We look at is a testing Force which ultimately pushes you to overcome. These forces show the weak links in our armor and are actually helping humanity to progress through sheer cussedness. The Shiva Shakti at work.

Janice Miller - Interesting! So, when Gandhi and Jesus were murdered, it was the testing Force pushing them out of the material world - an action which underscored their goodness and progress humanity as a whole. Reasonable assumption?

Pradeep Pk Maheshwari - No. They did not know when to stop. This is a very hidden angle. Humanity does not recognise it as yet. They were now sowing seeds that would create Chaos later. The Crusades. Inquisition, The partition of India, etc are the result of too much. Another Example is Napoleon Bonaparte. The wise ones know when to stop.

Evolution is taking place in a spiral (although looks like a circle). Every time a cycle is completed, things have gone up a notch.

Janice Miller - Makes sense. So when Jesus & Gandhi were murdered it was because they didn't know when to stop pushing their message? The message got too big and people either misunderstood it, or started using it and twisting it to their advantage. Is that what you mean? American schools taught that Napoleon was a bad guy, so you'll have to fill me in on why he was an example. I hate it that despite 3 degrees, my education is tarnished by political sway

Pradeep: - Janice, thank you for coming back on this and according me this respect and regard to pay me this attention.

About Gandhi/Jesus and many others - Yes. Jesus was here to add the element of Compassion into the atmosphere that was being influenced by the Roman military machine and the animal physical mentality of that period. Had he been (politically) understanding enough, he would not have stepped on toes so that they feel threatened. By becoming a martyr, he gave some very clever people good reasons to deify him and use him for their own nefarious purpose. With all his wisdom he did not know when to withdraw and when to go ahead. His job was to sow the seed and not become the tree.

Gandhi, was a good man at heart. But he was being converted into a God in his lifetime. Resisting the British was one thing but to understand the political climate of those times was another. Indians are very lethargic and his job was to wake them up but he should have withdrawn then and not become the political head. He let his Hindu conditioning and preference for Nehru as a person (who was a good man but not the right one to manage the country), interfere and his decisions played havoc and this divided the country and Pakistan is still at war with us - for no reason. He played into the hands of the political maneuvering.

Napoleon Bonaparte was a genius but he could not control his lust for absolute power. He put into action certain measures that eventually saw the growth of France into a major power. Like building canals all over France for navigation and transport, certain tax reforms etc. But he stepped again on many toes and the combined hate ended him. He was desperately trying to please a woman who couldn't care a whit for him. The woman who cared for him and would kept him on a happy and compassionate path of life later became the Queen of Sweden and her progeny still rule.

People who come as instruments always come as a flash in the pan for a short duration. They get something moving (sow the seed) and often although they may "look" wise, (Demonic forces are very wise as they are simply mirror images of the Divine) they get a foothold into the evolutionary pattern on this earth and create or destroy apparently at the same time. Their job is to shake things up. Remove the stagnating waters and renew the upward spiral of humanity's growth which the humans try hard to keep at a status quo.

Most wars and decimation of old cultures have this pattern behind them.

I give you names of other wiser people who have influenced life on earth but they were wise enough to stay out of the political controversies - Mark Twain, Bertrand Russell, Albert Einstein, Sri Aurobindo and many such others.

Janice Miller - The world needs governments specifically to organize and maintain municipal services, and create the ground rules for business dealings with other governments, whether it be government to government, government to business/person, or business/person to business/person. It seems to me that the leaders of most governments get drunk with power and forget the limits of their functions as a public servant.

I'm gathering that the demonic forces you mention are drawn to politics.

Could it be that the next evolution of society will remove the royalty status of political leaders and place them where they belong - as employees of a government paid for by the people's taxes? Or would such a suggestion reveal a lack of wisdom similar to that of Jesus, Gandhi, and the rest?

Where did you get such wisdom, Pradeep?

Pradeep - The next evolution will raise the conscious levels of humanity as a whole. Then good governance will come like a flower blooming. They will do the correct thing because their natures are so.

Janice Miller - That these days so many politicians are putting religion at the forefront is a bit unnerving - particularly as an excuse for war. You are very wise, Pradeep. I am honored to have you as a friend.

Pradeep - I am grateful

Religion is and always has been a good reason to create stampedes and fear in humanity. Rarely are there any good thoughts behind the decisions of politicians

We need to study more the lives of really great people like Talleyrand, Machiavelli, Chanakya, Confucius (and many more) to understand what is needed to administer well. These people all came in difficult times and helped navigate their rulers and their country by maintaining a wise balance and ruling through their kings. Never coming in the forefront. They were demi gods. Of course there are many others who ruled from behind but not wisely and were worse than bad rulers.

To beat these forces? - You can't beat them. These forces are primeval, all pervasive and run the things on earth.

There is a Divine being behind this game so things will always be Divine in the final analysis.

But what happens is that the teachers change as you grow. And your perceptions and reactions change so basically it is all a transformation taking place and every human or creature is at a different level and co existing.

You are safest when you stay with people of your own kind or on a higher plane. It is all a question of vibrations that you surround with.

You will get one of the three responses when you write about your life and thinking.

1) "What a Bummer". People will contradict you or explain to you the correct thinking or decide you are plain wrong and leave you alone.

2) Further Judge you, mostly derisively, on the basis of prejudices already loaded in their minds.

Example: " Oh he is now trying to white-wash his image/ what a show-off".

We have this saying in India - After eating 100 mice, the cat decides to go on pilgrimage.

3) Appreciation such as "oh he is so wise". This is what you have been dreaming to read/hear. But it happens rarely if at all.

True. I have seen the people who need help the most are the ones that runaway the fastest. Their own sense of self-importance is the barrier.

How about adding a little generosity, care-freeness and wild hugs into the mix?

Humans are funny. Humans want relationships but are afraid of the loss they will incur by joining hands. This I speak of related to all our close relationships; be it in personal lives or business. We do everything from the angle of: do I really need to? What is in it for me? What if he takes all the credit? What if they steal my thunder? How can I prevent my partner and friends do not end up getting a bigger share of the pie? Now please don't come at me saying the usual that I am very negative in my portrayal of humans. I personally think humans have painted themselves in too much positivity into a corner.

I have had the good luck of living with all kinds of people. From Living Gods to the downright cruel and criminal.

I am no angel either. But the kind people were so many and much more and the picture of what happens when we are cruel was so stark and forbidding that it washed my soul.

I feel that on a scale of 0 to 100 there are 0-10 who are basically cruel. 10-30 are moderately cruel and they let out their cruelty as and when they can. 30 - 50 are the average Joes who are equally primed depending on what goads them but they keep their cruelty exhibitions in control as they fear repercussions. In the 50-70 brackets they are basically kind but can be harsh when unduly provoked. 70-

90 are basically kind hate to be involved in any kind of show of cruelty or situation. 90-100 are the kind who is not only kind but they cannot be anything else.

This would all look like statistics with no meaning. But think – in marriage, in the child to parent relationships, bosses taking advantage of position how the world can becomes an arena of continuous cruelty for some – and they not knowing how to get out of it or fight back.

Millions of minds and as many numbers of interpretation. Everyone sure that they have understood it.

We talk to each other but never agree. I wonder why we talk at all.

Refuting is a useless exercise. It changes nothing in the minds of others. It adds a lot of resentment if anything.

Have you met anybody who takes credit for everything that is being done around him? He always was the one who did it. He is always the one who spent it. Had not been for him nothing would ever be done.

And of course he is never in error and nothing can be explained to him.

He will refute every word said and lose his temper and find much to quarrel about if confronted.

The kind of person who can only be avoided.

I had gone back to the Ashram after (55 yrs ago) my stint with parents and illness and told my Didi (elder sister/I had attached myself to) that I had learnt a lot in the interim period about people and the world.

She asked me back "Has this reduced your Ahankar (arrogance)?" The question perplexed me no end. I saw a dynamic me and this arrogance part was not at all visible.

But this question became important and I was thinking about it all the time.

Then later some 40 years ago my friend Lars from Denmark remarked that I was always speaking of negativity and criticising. This time I made the connection.

When we are finding fault with life around us, no doubt we are being observant but we are also projecting a picture of a "KNOW-IT-ALL". This puts the other person either to shame or in a position to defend or argue. There is one-upmanship too.

I observed this clearly in me; something that I had unknowingly imbibed by my Indian-ness. Now i see it all around me all the time and am vexed but keep aloof and out of society's dramatics.

I am so sad in the way we raise our children, talking to them always with a critical point as a sting in the tail in every conversation.
In social life we use it as excuse to pour out our violence in the most possibly worst ways like, lynching, bride burning, torturing children to work, rapes and murder.

The cruelty of Modern medicine or/and the lack of it. (Why are we so intent on keeping seriously sick people alive? Are we not over populated as it is?)

The very word "side-effects" should make our eyes pop.
How can this be when it is medicine and given for healing?
In some cases in the world administrations are using the law to enforce treatment like chemo. How can this be medicine?
See how the Unholy trinity of Food processors, Drug producers & Enforcers work together to make money out of

the human misery. I give just one example.

Knowingly the food processing industry brainwashed the public to adopt trans-fat oils that have no nutrition value and end up clogging the humans system. It is one of the prime reasons for our accelerating problem of obesity, diabetes and heart attacks. The industrial processing actually renders it into slow poison. But no one is prepared to look into this. They did the same to sugar and allowed the humans to start consuming sugar as a "drug" in quantities 6 to 10 times the normal. How is this acceptable? Then the doctors come in. Without understanding the individual or even wanting to they treat him as they would repair a car or such machine. They think of mechanical answers to diseased state like "heart attacks". We have stents, by-passes and heart transplants which are huge money-making activities. The insurance philosophy has impoverished our thinking to a point where we don't care as long as we don't have to spend anything on treatment because clearly health is not our problem. The Doctor knows best and he is always there on call.

Modern society is sort-sighted and looks for scape-goat answers.

They blame smoking and alcohol and immediately put a dead stop to it all. This results in extra trauma to the body that is habituated to it and its chemistry is totally organized around the bad habits. How come the doctors have not understood that this is bad practice and the change needs to be gradual at best; anyway the psychological factors HAVE TO BE taken into account. But no; the patient does not matter.

The "appearances" are more important.

The protocol devised by the clever brains in administration decides and the law has to be followed. The patient is not important.
You see we as humans were never important to them; only as fodder to their greed.
But yet we have come to define "Doctors" as know-all and are trusted implicitly when it concerns "OUR" health. Of course even in this bad system there are good people but they have been conditioned and taught wrong.
I have seen so many people dying because of bad advice. Just imagine the number of deaths that today are documented due to faulty medication and prescribing. How can a safe, properly researched medical system have such high figures? And all the other deaths that happen because of bad nutrition and habits that the doctors suddenly interfere with? These are unfortunately not into taken into account as they are not seen as results from medical intervention.

Take this case. An unhappy person who has responsibly taken care of his entire family of his own and brothers and sisters eventually takes to drink; takes tobacco too and eats rather difficult to digest foods. Over the years his chemistry has adapted to his life style but gradually he is becoming sick or let us call it simple "fatigued". Deep in his heart he has stopped caring. He has a mild heart attack and the entire medical intervention puts a stop to all his support system, the family supports the medical troupe. Now he is in pain due to the withdrawal and unhappy 6 times over as the family too is against him. His pain is not acknowledged by anyone. It is a tragedy. Soon his heart fails him and he is no more. (I saw it coming and tried to advise against following this line of thought and action but I was too small a fry)

How did all this help?

Do you realize that the modern medicine is not curing you and advising you correctly to correct the disease-path you have chosen to live with but helping you survive a bit a longer by actually promoting your life style? A life style that is hurting you that psychologically you don't wish to change. My philosophy is that we should let sleeping dogs be and if they are so intent to killing themselves, let them be. Give advice but do not enforce it. The problem as I see it is that their advice is also faulty. And give advice only when asked three times at least.

Have you ever tried to advice anyone against binge TV watching, late nights, over-doing the alcohol, salt and sugar, fried or factory processed and chemical laden foods? You would realize how impossible a task it all is.

Look at the way diabetes is touching all lives. We feel that insulin added to the body is solving the problem. No; it is delaying the inevitable…. a more horrific inevitable like kidney failure or collapse of the heart. The answer is in self-control and change of eating habits. If we did not give them the solution of insulin they would be forced to live a better life-style by changing their habits. But "no"; with insulin available they feel safe to pursue their life style and get sicklier in the long run.

Look how much relief steroids bring. We get used to the steroids. They are the perfect answer to our prayers. We continue merrily till the steroids kill us.

And so on and so forth.

Hiding behind masks.

In the formal and capsuled environment of today we are training the minds to think linear and "ACCEPT" certain given parameters and ingest facts as ordained. It is even backed by law to think in a particular way. Non-acceptance of dictates invites punishment.

Is this conducive to "Learning"? NO?

This is creating the highly informed and computerized "personas" of today that are totally useless in an emergency, cannot and don't want to even think beyond the socially accepted norms.

This way of BEING suits the commercial world which is increasingly controlling governance. Personal needs, liberties and liabilities have been thrown to the wind.

Individuality is looked down upon as it has been since the beginning of time but now it is easy to enforce and spread because of education having gone large scale and customized. By coupling the education with Government approved Certificates and then making the Certificates the platform of all activities like running a school or teaching or stating an industry, the establishment has effectively produced robots who pay also pay for it to become it.

See how in the final analysis people now think and behave.

Fashions are dictated by industry. Psychology is dictated by the practice of psychiatry. Medicine is either TRUE or fake.

Mother Nature and personal experience has been trashed.

We do what others expect. We want only what others think is valuable.

The mass control and authority that was first intimated by The Romans is now today a reality. "It has gone so deep into the basic human sub-consciousness that it has given to birth to a special kind of character – "Some people are so virtuous that they make it their life's work to fault others or find errors."

Take for instance the beauty industry. The commonality of thinking what is considered beautiful is astounding to me to say the least.

In a school gathering of my daughter's class I was rather numbed into a kind of shock on seeing the faces. All the mothers looked like alabaster marble busts with moving eyes.

What kind of cosmetic beauty make-up is this? Is this today's idea of looking superbly smooth everlasting young? I had difficulty in recognizing which one was which. They looked the same to me and I thought, God, has the museum from Florence walked into this room?

What culture is this that prides itself in hiding itself so thoroughly - Inert and lifeless?

Behind 99% of marriages is the Greed for Dowry.

Behind many of the cruelties in married life is the greed to blackmail HER father for evermore.

Her beauty, education and companionship rarely are the issue.

It is always how much dowry she is bringing in and how much she can bring as an employed woman or her value as a servant in the home.

NB: Forget never; all cats are grey in the dark.

Shannon Lee McGillion: ...99 ! %

What does the world know? We are not a nice lot. Believe me

Does anyone ever really peep into the male spirit?

What do they see in the female of the species?

In the west people marry for passionate reasons and the marriages don't last.

In the east we marry for every other reason but passionate attraction to a particular woman. We rarely are given an opportunity by society.

In both cases marriages exist as the world does not offer any respite or options otherwise. Romantic dreams are never satisfied. So we have a disgruntled dysfunctional society.

It is easy to understand the marriages of young people failing because the hormones initiated them.

I have so often said that marriage should be after the age of at least 35 and divorce not allowed when there are children to care for.

Malachy Matthews: So Pradeep, if what the post says is generally true in India (which I am finding hard to swallow), do prospective brides not see through the system and resent being a lottery scratch-card? What's in it for them?

I'm asking on the basis that all humans are self-interested, not just the male in the marriage.

Pradeep PK: Women had no choice. Even the young men/boys had very little choice. Alliances were and mostly even now made on the basis of the wishes of elders/parents. Though I may sound like exaggerating a little to give this point a bit of extra flavour, the children in the marriage had little or no choice. The arrangements were always based on family status, caste, financial and political aspirations. Astrology played also a part.

As most young people had no idea of any relationship with the opposite sex or the world, it worked as there was nothing in their minds or memories to think or desire differently. Hormones demanded attention that is all. The brain was trained to think that way from day one.

Mostly a good relationship would eventually develop between the couples. Of course the opening up of society in the last fifty years has made some difference in the professional families.

What are the chances of this world, its people and the general behavior will change?

None.

It can't. It is like gravity. Unidirectional. With new births every second with trained humans dying with non-transferable memories, this world cannot be corrected in any degree in any sense.

Only Mother Nature can and She is doing at the rate of few feet every million years.

....

Malachy Matthews Lol I love that about trained humans dying all the time! At 60 I am now considered to be 'over the hill' in terms of the capacity in which I used to work. What they don't get is that it is only now that I have reached my best and can give the most, based on my experience and mistakes. So they take on 30 year olds who will make serious mistakes that will affect their business. No, humanity is unlikely to learn. And Ageism is a mountainous stumbling block. It's quite shocking and surprising really that obvious skills in older people are ignored by organisations who want to make a profit. Or perhaps they know that they can't foist their corporate BS on me because I will tell them to feck off and leave the door swinging behind me!

Pradeep Pk Maheshwari

Accurately said to T

By social standard I should not speak about it but I have seen most proprietors of business etc are either self-made people with limited training or understanding of the world but having expertise in one particular field and of course those who come into money and readymade businesses.

In my life there were many in family and family connections who would see the talent in me but were afraid that I may overwhelm their own personas so I would not be really welcome even when they knew I would be highly profitable to their work.

They wanted me as a quiet servant which was simply a no go for me.

...

Kaela Bedard to Pradeep Pk Maheshwari that's a pretty negative point of view. I understand why you think that, but if we change ourselves and show change is possible, more people will follow. We just have to lead and prove anything is possible.

Pradeep Pk Maheshwari Why would anyone follow? Whatever for? When we change, do others see any change in our fortunes or status due to it? What interest they may have?

Kaela Bedard Of course, we can't change them, they have to do that, but if we explain our experiences, even if we only get one person to help, that's still one more person who is self-aware and willing to change.

Pradeep Pk Maheshwari to Kaela Bedard ...And then we all die. The world goes on and repeats itself sine die.

Agreeing with you will reduce my stature in the eyes of the world.

We have reached the basest level of any educated society that has ever reached...... sadly these are the people with tummies full, comfortable warm beds.

Humans are as yet not ready for "plenty", it has only raised the head of the serpent.

Ease of life has only made them malevolent.

So this conclusion: Wise ones exist only because there are these contradicting coyotes and dancing peacocks to spice our lives. I feel that this contradicting attitude and the dance they do and the dance they lead us does finally egg on some of us to not take it sitting down but find ways means to escape. In the final metamorphosis it is a spiritual act as every annoying thing on this earth is.

As for the act of contradicting and taking the opposite stance? It soon becomes a habit. They contradict or find fault because they have become so – an automaton. Their brains are full of connecting images or phrases to the words you may have used and it is this association of words and images, with the support of their vanities that creates this scenario.

Contradicting is so easy; so much fun to see the shock in the eyes of others and so comforting to know that we were able to shut-up & put somebody down with just a few words.

It is quite simply our inferiority complex showing up as The Superior. It is a dare to the world in general and to you that if you have the courage to fight back let us see if you would throw it all into the wind and kill the relationship.

It is one way of testing the waters of telling you off and saying that you are really not needed here to complete the relationship.

Most people, down with their egos hurt, start explaining themselves.

The wise ones see the ensuing battle and quietly walk off - let the other live in his/her grand scheme of things.

Fate, Men and women

Fate:

Judy Lester: And what is fate? Destiny? Fate negates any free will.

Pradeep Pk Maheshwari: Fate is the one that gives you the Free Will and then the opportunities to use it.

The negation comes from our ignorance, arrogance and laziness.

Judy Lester: Why does fate give me free Will?

Pradeep Pk Maheshwari: To use it and see what will happen. It is a way of adding some personal responsibility in the universal affairs. It is also a clean method of helping individuals realise how fallible our understanding and abilities really are. This is why failure is thought of as a teacher and hence the expression "Experience is the best teacher".

There is an ambiguous problem in the understanding of FATE. Some like the Hindus live in the delusion that we have no say in the matter of conducting our lives. They are therefore defeatist and mentally then live a retarded life looking for answers in the stars and curing their ills thru ceremonies in temples to please the gods. It is a kind of escapism.

The western psyche is the opposite. They have this feeling that they are in total control and they are the ones that make things happen. This also gives them the right to lord over all beings with the power of life and death. This is pure arrogance but swords and bullets fly without restraint.

Whatever,

As if Truth happily living in the Realm of Gods really could care. It is forever laughing under its mask.

The reality as I tend to tell it is: there is a Universal flow in which we are just a part, a small cog in a huge operation. And we enter this operation for a miniscule moment - like a drop in a flowing river.

The poor drop. But often it is given a choice and this is what determines if it will land in the sea or a pond. Such as if it goes left of the rock in the way or right.

And to sum it up you know well that fate does not give us free will but choice of saying Yes or No into a moment where the story is already laid out for us. Each moment in life we are met with a question and how we respond to it is what takes our lives forward.

Every thought, action counts. This is the basic principle of karma.

My first question is how much influence does the average human have in how humanity and FATE will play their games on Earth?

If Nostradamus could predict events hundreds of years ago, it goes to reason that there is a process and formula at work which makes certain events and activities quite the norm as one step following the other while walking.

But humans live in the bubble in the now and think with great pride that they are running things.

And from the results we are producing, I would say our pride and priorities are badly misplaced.

Every kid has a neatly laid out spiritual destiny and his learning will go along with it.

Real good teaching should be able to direct the kid accordingly.

But we digress.

The basic concept of present day schooling methods developed in the 19the century when the need was for soldiers and clerks to create empires. The same mentality continues today when new types of empires are being made. We really do not want thinking adults and creative to boot. It would defeat the entire commercial establishment.

The internet changed many things. It took the minds of people in many directions so now the leaders and the led are both like confused tribesmen in a forest when their forests are cut down.

The old school is clamping down as we can see with information "blocks" being put in place and fake news or manipulated news is fed to the netizens.

So many wrong practices are in place that I wonder if things can ever really get better at the "Crowd" level because the crowd has only shown a tendency to fall toward a lowering of consciousness. At least for the moment.

The Demons have played their cards supremely well.

From the Spiritual Destiny angle, nothing ever goes waste. Even the mental interference, mental blocks and Detours that result from human mental interference. There is delay but the process is toughened and results in greater, more thorough and better job done in the final analysis.

Yes this is normally what happens. The lucky ones get such a beating from life that they end up discovering HUMILITY and connect with intelligence again.

We all, without exception suffer from this. All of us practice some activity that we consider spiritual/superior and give ourselves credit and values out of proportion to the activity which possibly has merit only in our minds. Our self importance and grandness then overpowers our thinking

The path is whatever comes next and the exigency that crops up. We don't know the path and neither do we really know the destination. Things will happen in their time and at their pace as one step following the other while walking.

The truth is that wheels are turning and blocks are falling and I can use good company

Men/women

The word "LOVE" means Dissolve in the Divine to love of coffee to plain sex. It all depends on the level of consciousness one is at.

So this word has really no meaning. It is the most used and misunderstood word in the English language.

About humans and as I see it in humans it is basically a selfish movement although for a while one does get into the right spirit of it.

Men and women; we really live very separate (oil & water mix) lives but this concept of "love" has us hoodwinked.

You give a shake and there is a semblance of mixing. You stop and things settle down to both being their individualistic selves – refusing to integrate.

So I presume that humans love needs effort, continuous practice of deliberate effort in thought and action to be LESS Selfish, More considerate and using our intelligence to understand and learn to being better at it.

Do your realize that this is raj Yoga - The spiritual path to emancipation?

Kimberly Rasmussen: It's really amazing if you can figure out how to deal with the opposites it hands you. Not an easy feat. Best of both worlds. I think you can be whole as an individual and have an entire new wholeness as the two wholes come together. It really is magical. My husband and I have come so far.

Pradeep Pk Maheshwari: Agree Kimberly Rasmussen. But from the personal it needs to grow into the Universal. That is when it will realise itself in its full grandeur.

Kimberly Rasmussen: Pradeep tell me more please. How do you go from personal to universal?

Parris Ja Young: Ah ha! We can forget the higher forms and consider sexual love alone! It is so powerful. I am not talking indulgent sex, I am talking loving sex. I am talking sex that connects first as chemistry. Pow! Two are drawn together. If, with the gentlest nudge of the Great Mystery, that love rises to Eros, then there is a joining of spheres ... and the winning of a crown.

Here in the USA folks develop a condition where their spirits exist within a glass-like bubble. We are isolated and alone, although we form relationships. When love happens, portions of our "bubbles" merge; a THIRD being arises, a being you and your beloved share. Sometimes that overlap becomes a wedge, because the one, whose self-awareness is improved through the degree at which they can see through the eyes of another, may hate what they see. Or they may love what they see and grow to become the animus or anima to the other. Such states DO EXIST and are of great value.

Kimberly Rasmussen: Parris I didn't know you can become the anima or animus. How is this possible?

Pradeep Pk Maheshwari: Kimberly Rasmussen When put this way it sounds funny. But Parris Ja Young is right. We absorb the vibes of others and when we are in long drawn associations, we start vibrating to others and vice versa.

Particularly in sexual relations with intense passion the transfer is on a very high transformative scale

Pradeep Pk Maheshwari: There comes a time when we sincerely realise that our human "love" is an interdependent arrangement in which our imagination plays a big part. We keep each other interested in each other by inflating the Ego.

It becomes Universal when we see it in action all around us and start noticing the little glitches in the pretended relationships that are based more on habits of a comfort zone that we build around us.

Once we see this, we start also seeing that there is enough genuine kindness and compassion in us and everybody else.... hidden away by selfish motives and considerations backed by our arrogance/pride/vanity.

Then it is something that becomes obvious when you realise that others won't let you in into their cozy zones and that fences have been put up. We try to hide these fences by certain words and activities that have been labeled as indicators of "lovingness".

It is all a sham.

The hardest part is in realising that we are actually very cruel in our basic make-up

For Success, you need Detachment.

 I have always felt that the attitude/philosophy with which children are brought up has more of a role to play in the way health-wise and ability wise the children will come out. We had doubts and we went out to learn before we started.

But the poor stress more on their pride and very arrogantly disdain to confront the subject.

Almost everything depends on the few "thoughts: and "Emotional responses/habits" on the foundations of which we grow up into LIFE.

The poor are poor because they spend on their "image" more than doing something about it.

I have heard this so often that I now have given up: ...What is wrong with our life? We eat and live well", "What is wrong with the way we are bringing up our children?", "You think you are better than us?".....all aggressive questions designed to shut up any thinking on the subject.

They are promoting brands and high priced junks more than the rich.

The rich spend on essentials and on the goals of their lives.

I find more laborers, living in hovels with no overheads like taxes and huge rents to worry about, spending small fortunes on hair styling and Adidas/Reebok shoes. They then very soon burden themselves with family and children and get trapped in the "Chkravyuh" (LABYRINTH/Maze) of life, never to get out of it again.

The middle-class, when they come into some money do the same except that their first focus is on the biggest SUV and ridiculous Designer clothes- nothing less will let them feel unashamed to go out in public.

Suffering happens when we stop the learning process. One example: Every intelligent person to whom I explained that the use of industrially processed cooking oils is doing major damage, quickly switched over to healthier alternative. But the ones who are destined to suffer scoffed it vehemently. The same with information imparted on the formula of Coke, Energy drinks etc. Or any other subject for that matter.

Worse by not taking responsibility for their lives (it is so much easier to grumble and blame other factors) they fall into the clutches of charlatan degree holders who take all their money and leave them suffering even more.

I see people going for expensive courses that bring them nothing in terms of knowledge or abilities but hope and regret in plenty. BUT then as friend Ken Timper says: Did they make some less than perfect decisions in the past? Did YOU?? Pride and arrogance always go together.

Things started worsening with the coming of the TV. This system of brainwashing needs to be closed before any improvement can be discussed.

The people were so easily netted, that in the realm of the wise, it would be termed as "ludicrous".

A lot of people start with the thought that it is their karma and their life. And before they have learnt any skill or trade or created any source of livelihood they start having children who eat away whatever little there is. They trap themselves in perpetual poverty with an attitude to boot.

Life demands effort to crawl out from under the rock of tamas, mental laziness and inertia. A very great many people just do not want to.

(Which often makes me conclude that it is their destiny and choices made by their souls and best is to leave them alone and wait for them to ask for help which in their pride they may never do. Often they do ask for help but as doles not "opportunities")

I have tried to help a lot of people working for me help them rise higher and tried to raise their level of thinking to help their children get better openings - not one parent took my help in the last 40 years.

Of course - speaking generally.

We shall see change when we go one step further by becoming more aware ourselves and note objectively the true value of a person by

1) VIBES being emanated.

We normally miss this because we are being taught to disregard our intuitive sense. All Beings emanate certain vibes of their guiding principal thoughts – such as generosity or thieving. It will also show in their words and clothes and how they tell their stories. We know all this but we do not expressly directly teach it to our children - As if living a lie is a virtue.

To see life as it is, our children are dependent on audio-visual inputs like movies, videos that can do a lot of good till it was limited to great movies but are now streaming all the time with the aim to unfortunately do the opposite as if the controlling powers behind the scene have decided that uplifting of the human race is not be permitted.

2) MENTAL acuity being shown.

People normally close their minds and become more involved in proving themselves after a certain age. They get so involved with their own image that they stop listening and learning – even from experience/incidents. They protect themselves by refusing to open themselves to new ideas and possibilities. It is easy to recognize this. By their words and body language they show exactly their state of mind. Most of us are downright so negative that NOs & NOTs and exaggerated reasons will be put forward and a lot of energy spent in arguing to avoid all possibilities of a shift in stance.

The human race will go forward once this block is recognized and not allowed and we take the extra effort to teach it to our children.

....

Please don't look for deep arguments in what I say above.

The idea is more to get people thinking and if possible to change a little their attitude to become more open and generous in their thinking.

But it is all talk finally.

In his memoirs, Barrack Obama writes about Rahul Gandhi:

"Rahul Gandhi has 'a nervous, unformed quality about him, as if he were a student who'd done the coursework and was eager to impress the teacher but deep down lacked either the aptitude or the passion to master the subject."

PK: I would say this is the condition of half our youths.

As they are mollycoddled and baby-fed while the fathers run tightly controlled jurisdiction with no awareness that one day the children will have to confront the world and we have to prepare them for the future.

Unfortunately at the same time these kids are fed stories that being their child they have achieved greatness already and nothing further is required.

We are manufacturing nincompoops who are basically cads and can be very violent and vindictive too.

Respond with controlled intent. To be successful.

Nothing in this life is more confusing than people who respond with intent.

We normally expect people to react in a particular pattern that is particular to each of us; something that we understand about each other after a few meetings. We then pattern our advances to suit the needs of the moment with calculated behavior from our side to make certain that the other person responds in a given manner as desired by us.

People are generally a cluster of habits, philosophy and they respond within an established frame-work that they call "ME". This is easily read and manipulated. Most of us are so enclosed in a habitual pattern that it is impossible to reach us on any other platform as we become closed entities and therefore predictable and immediately labeled as useless or useful and on the basis of this label kept away or made friends with. A lot of effort goes in these manipulations.

But the mind can be educated to rise above the instinctual and operate with controlled reason and the behavior patterns reigned in with will power and intent. People who learn to do this use all the information at their disposal and all the learning from their experiences to act, and respond. It is all a very controlled act. They are normally read all wrong and they are not predictable because they play life as a chess game. This is the secret of success in this world.

Project yourself with intent. We do this naturally only when we are wooing. It may be any kind of wooing; for attention by a partner, or a job, to get discounts or any such interest of very personal benefit. We need to rise a step or two higher and learn to think and "do". And as far as possible think well and act with kindness.

Compare the way James Bond responds to people and situations with the people in general. The intent and my words will become so totally clear.

James Bond should be seen as a yogi. A YOGI is someone who responds with intent. A YOGI is not the guy-in-the-street. He has mastered his reactions and responses or at least he is on the way to do so. It is difficult to gauge him for more often than not he deliberately gives out wrong signals to avoid people and situations of no interest to him.

In my Opinion.

The phrase "in my opinion..." is one of the emptiest, devoid of meaning or sense - phrase. For the simple reason that one's opinion has really meaning to the speaker and often I wonder if even this true.

We are all living in a bubble of our personal emancipation. We are a packet of second-hand information/knowledge rarely coming out of our own learning thru experience, trial and tribulations.

"Our opinion" has no direct silk thread to reality or another's reality. It is a vague picture in our mind, like a dream couched in words and srt5rung out like a story that seems sensible, logical and relatively sane.

Then what are we harping about?

This is the way men create drama and self-importance for themselves.

This world is an amusement park. Just sit in your rocking chair and enjoy the show.

The sadness is in the part that the episodes are repetitive and predictable.

You are trying to reach minds that are locked up. Emotional responses rule our decisions. Useless.

I just had a muffin of the mass factory produced variety. I keep them for emergencies when I need something to eat urgently.

And I was thinking:

We have foods that do not feed.

We have speeds that take us nowhere.

We have telephony that has speech that says nothing.

It is advancement towards NOTHING. Buddha would be pleased.

When your thoughts and wishes become clear-cut, the solution will come in response. Normally our thoughts are not fully formed and have yet to take shape because we have not resolved our demons and desires. Without a clear-cut agenda to pursue, nothing can manifest.

If you are not succeeding, look at your thoughts. Can you put your goal or your idea in clear cut writing (Let us say) in 20 words?

The problem of and Question of Commitment.

Why are we so weak on commitments?

This is where the ills of humanity begin. We are for some reason made this way. Call it whatever name like Bluffing, Lying or cheating the fact remains that our foundation is shaky and we speak without intent. The philosophers call it INSINCERITY but it is more than that.

Humans make statements, Commitments based on the mood of the moment. Tomorrow is another day. This the psychological truth our natures and general character but we do not accept it as we project ourselves as sincere, honest and indulging people; something that we are not. There are different grades of concentration of sincerity in this; every individual being at a different level. Some are absolutely insincere from the day go and are non-corrigible and there are others who are basically sincere and honest but sometimes life's weight and strain can be too much and they have to break their vows and they do so involuntarily with a heavy heart but necessity can be a hard master.

The point I wish to make is that humanity has no future unless and until it starts taking its commitments seriously. Every word we utter has to be with intent and act as written in stone. Once "in" we are in and there can be no way to wriggle out of the commitment and arrangement.

You marry; you stay married. You have children you stay put and see to it that they mature well and get ready for life onward. You quote a price and delivery; you do it. You take a job; you deliver. You give a job; you become responsible for the person. You make a promise; you don't forget it. You make a mistake; you acknowledge it. When somebody stands by you; you don't ever forget it and remain in debt forever.

Humans need to stand by each other otherwise this world as it is, painful, unreliable and a torment to existence will remain as it is. All our talks of God, philosophy, Ethics are simply ripples on the surface of the pond; meaningless waste of time and energy and resources – as we see these practices in operation, they are all charades based on our insincere dramatic abilities.

Nothing at all is going to ever ease the burden of living whatever the comfort level we achieve thru technology and policing. Just like cockroaches cannot be policed or controlled nothing can be done unless we first start policing ourselves.

Those who will not discipline themselves by "THOUGHT" need FEAR to exercise control.

There seems to be no other way. How easily good solutions turn into "evil" harbingers is surprising and almost always certain.

Study the subject of contraception. The Sexual energy in Nature is far stronger than the mental discipline humans are very able to impose upon themselves. Occult Tantric Psychology tells us that it is presently the strongest most powerful energy active on Earth and when used judiciously it is life giving but it is also highly conducive to the carrier of diseased forces that enter through it like viruses and embed themselves into the body as incurable sickness, fatigue and depletion of nervous strength.

So intelligent, farsighted humans devised and organized the society we have today in which unwanted pregnancies outside marriage or even in marriage were made taboo.

But the clever human with its intelligence found ways and means to almost certainly stop the pregnancies without needing to stop the sexual stimuli. Humanity has gone mad with its unbridled hunger for sex which never seems to get satisfied bringing with it loss of self-discipline, sickness and fatigue and the joy of togetherness is gone giving way to depression.

The human persona cannot live or survive in a continuous perpetual state of excitement which it is trying to do now and only ending up being sick or depressed.

There are Two Hearts.

The Human Persona is Double Layered. We are really two people in one external form. It is a mere sense of perception that separates the two Beings.

Look at how the Poet sees it all: What "is" you?

You are but your BREADTH. The day you stop breathing you become dust and are thrown back into bosom of Mother Earth to be recycled.

There is this physical form; complete in itself with its own heart and mind which we normally know as instinct. This is the basic animal that we all are. Given form by the cellular activity in Nature. We are not different from most being on earth except that in the human form another Element has been added – what Sri Aurobindo calls the Psychic Being.

So we have this body with its instinctive Desires and Basic Thinking Apparatus. At the same time there is also this Psychic Being with its own Emotional Centre and Thinking Apparatus.

Most quarrels on Earth begin when these two clash due to the Physical Mind calling its instinctive process with the same words as that are applied to the Psychic Being. The separateness not having been duly established and recognized as yet.

So we have two hearts, two minds and two souls. Once we look at it this way the confusion clears.

What the physical body calls love shows in a Physical Form is the Baby making machinery. The same word Love is used for the Generous Being that has roots in the Psychic being.

The organ called heart is also synonymous with the feeling of self-less affection.

The word MIND is also connected to the Brain with its nervous system and intricate memory bank and habits etc; the psychic Being is also talked of with the use of the word MIND but it totally another entity that is using the physical mind to express itself but should be best referred to as The INTUITIVE mind.

Most of the people on Earth are still very deeply connected and living at the Physical level. The vocabulary used is confusing and creating animosity in use. It is cleverly being used to confuse issues and when we use the same vocabulary to clear the issues we only end up generating more storms and unending arguments, which are normally called discussions yet are anything but.

So when we do not see eye to eye, we should take the above into consideration. We may be using the same words but not referring to the same things. We need to first accept that like the colour gray, there are 10001 shades between white and black. It is easy to get trapped in a maze of words with double meaning and "entendres".

This can be corrected somewhat by "reflecting and meditating" quietly before allowing ourselves to respond either vocally or silently or as often seen in with sheer violent physical force as of hurting the body will stop the minds from functioning. This rarely happens; actions and reactions follow each other in fast succession tied closely together as in a necklace. No wonder this earth is in a mess.

The process of Human Thought.

2 stories:|

1] The neighbors had placed their flower tree blocked on a corner because there was no place. So I said to myself, shall I offer them to keep it in front of my apartment. This way I'll enjoy the beauty of these flowers too and offer the plant a lifeline.

And as if they had heard me, they did place it in front of my apartment the next day.

2] The young lady who helps us in dusting/cleaning our place told me that the neighbors she works for were wondering greatly of how I live, what I do and how although I don't seem to anything I am so "Nose-up-in-the-air" and never seem to need others around me.

She told them that I do most of the repairs and work myself and I am quite a bit on the computer.

Ah they concluded he must be playing the share-market. (Something I would not touch with a barge pole). And that is that – I from my side conclude that this conclusion helps them to place me properly within the moneyed people bracket as they wouldn't like to be seen with poor neighbors!

Thérèse Lepage Lachapelle-Bhatnagar

In your PERSONAL life, have you realized how "some" people have absolutely NO interest in YOUR life? The minute you start talking about yourself, your family, your interests even if you've been paying attention, listening to them for an hour, they turn OFF, whether on the phone, in person, on Messenger, etc.!

These might be your family members, your best friends, on Facebook or in real life, your acquaintances, or anyone else!

Pradeep PK Maheshwari

Yes. Most people are like that. They learn early in life to shut off because of the continuous disturbance adults create in their lives since the day they learn to move about. Children get so tired of being asked to do this, being lectured or not being allowed to do that. In school the continuous barrage of instructions is spiritually shutting off and I have seen most teachers are not using kindness at all to regulate them.

In exasperation they soon learn to shut off and then it becomes a habit and part of their adult nature.

We, adults need to accept and understand that we are actually training children to become bad listeners - we over-use our authority to silence them in their growing up period and later they repay us in kind.

Unfortunately, the young adults do not realise that they have actually become so hearing-deficient and the wall they have created around them is keeping "LIFE" away from them.

They preempt others by doing the talking and keeping on talking, often meaninglessly.

In addition I must add that most people really do not have much of importance to say and are very boring indeed. Our social needs to listen to each other because we need each other can be a severe drain on our time and energies and spiritually speaking often leaves a dark cloud hovering over us.

This smart phone is such a boon.

"Try to make it work kindly and lovingly"

TOO MUCH REGULATION AND TOO MUCH TECHNOLOGY ARE BOTH KILLING THE HUMAN SOCIAL FABRIC.

They brought in minimum wages and a lot of employers stopped employing.

They brought in machinery and created unemployment and a society without money to buy their goods.

They gave them Appliances and communication tools and made them even lazier.

Thieving is easier than working for it so cheating got inadvertently promoted.

And then we gave them fast vehicles to steal and run and organize themselves from a distance thru cellphones.

What are we actually doing?

The humans are anti-intelligence.

We wish to survive without others around us but need workers to fulfill our needs and run our factories but we do not really want to pay for services yet when it is our own turn we insist on being paid for every little thing very high prices.

Is this sustainable?

Machinery and automation should have a simple purpose. To help the worker - not replace him.

Machinery should be permitted and adopted only where it can be concretely demonstrated in jobs that can be done better and more efficiently with mechanical help.

What you call your wealth is not yours. It belongs to Earth and you are here only for 3 score and 10 years or so.

Bring your hearts out into the open. Share and strive for contentment.

If you are special it will show.

We need each other.

But things were simpler, normal and natural before religious fanaticism entered the picture.

The error I feel though is in the legal system that enforces "possession".

Nothing in our social fabric today enforces "Try to make it work kindly and lovingly"

The source of our ANGER AND VIOLENCE:

Deep down our prejudices, our image of how our greatness requires to be treated and behaved with are the cause of irritation that can easily be magnified to show that we have been insulted or hurt and punishment from us to them is then justified so if we are in a position to get away with it, we let lose our temper with a little drama and a lot of impunity.

We spend the entire fun-time of our lives in boring schools. The only lesson finally that makes any sense is that nobody really cares; all are busy looking if others are looking at them. When it dawns on you that by the age of 20 with all your stunning looks, brilliant conversations, fabulous world-changing ideas and observations....only 20 or so people know about you, a rather greyish pall descends on you.

We opt for all the known methods of singling ourselves out in this crowded world. Some buy cars, some buy expensive out-fits and some make themselves obnoxious.

Let us stop for a moment and without worrying about it too much, let us look at life objectively. Go back just 150 years. Check-out some of the best long existing brands and how they promote themselves and why people are interested in them. The reasons: a] Real good quality, b] Expensive, c] Snob value and d] everyone knows about the exclusive nature of the product and its price tag. Example: Rolex and Rolls Royce.

In the new era of the last 30 years it is Apple phones and Nike shoes and Tees to match or as I now despondently see, clothes that are attention grabbing to the extreme by being purposely torn or see-thru.

The basic thing is to be seen with it and bask in the reflected glory of second looks that it brings.

But does it bring attention? Yes it does…..but the kind one does not want. Records show that robberies are rampant and the most flashy cars get stolen first, jealousy and envy can be seen in the eyes of all the aspiring working class, molesters target the most direct targets walking freely about and you cannot even walk on the streets or let your children out without a little fear in your heart due to all the negative news that you are bombarded with all the time.

In this pursuit we have only managed to degrade the Earth and soon by the time we reach fifty, we realize that we are not special by any means and nobody cares.

So the time to make something of life with the strength and energy that we had has passed and now with new wisdom we push on for really seeing life properly with values that matter such as kindness and cooperation. We are more at peace and ready to meet our eternal companion that is death for he is the only one with constant eyes on you.

What is the most prevalent emotion in mankind?

My answer: Anguish.

Before reacting to my reply, please reflect.

Most of us would think of Love and would jump to contradict this statement like the trained minds (monkey-minds) that we are.

Love is the strongest and most powerful emotional movement but the most prevalent is anguish. The Driving force of love cannot be contested but it is also the emotion that starts most of the cascading other emotions in us. Nothing in our lives brings more anguish than the concept of, the thought of, the idea of and the expectation of what we call Love.

Humans have not analysed themselves properly. What they call love is the primary motive force in Mother Nature to create more babies and there is an instinctive wave to it. All the species know what to do and how to take care of their babies and nurture them. But humans are more complex. To their persona is now added a mind that is a little separated from the instinctive mind.

This is the intellectual mind that can override the instinctive mind and this mind can be trained to operate in a given direction. How this mind will project itself eventually depends quite a bit the way it has been programmed in the early nascent stage of childhood. This is the general assumption. This is quite true but along with this there is also another factor at work and that is the basic nature that we were provided with when we are formed in the womb. It is rarely thought of but even the spiritual atmosphere at the time of conception leaves its mark. And one of the elements that form our persona is Pride.

This is the element that creates all the anguish in our lives. Humans have called it the Ego but really it is nothing but the simple fact that LIFE loves to be appreciated. It would have been a great boon because this emotion prompts us to appreciate others too. But we demand attention and do not understand why others don't appreciate us; the fact that others have their own axe to grind is lost on us. The flip side is resentment.

And we have much to resent too. One the most important resentment is the fact that instead if life flowing the way we want it to, it takes altogether in another direction and this is rarely happily accepted. Add insult to injury, we are normally forced to resign ourselves to accept it.

This is heavily resented although most of us can do really very little about it and we go about giving the impression that this is exactly what we had asked for. Resentments run deep; very very deep. WE may resent where we are born, into the society we are born into and the wealth and conditions piled on us and the pattern of behaviour imposed on us by this accident of birth. There is always so much to resent: why is one born to be king and the other a lowly peasant? Why do we have to do so many things in life against our wishes – why are we forced to conform and yet put up a brave face of being satisfied, content and superior? It is galling.

Al these questions weigh heavily upon us but we rarely ask or contemplate how we can live more efficiently so that our future generations may live happier. We are normally so focused on our own short joys that we destroy the fabric for later and often find ourselves deep in the morass before we are released by the inevitability of fate.

BUT WE CAN BLAME others and this can be the mitigating factor in our personal lives but also discharge negative emotions into the atmosphere. This permits us to feel good. Good enough to continue appreciating ourselves in the image of what we imaginatively see ourselves to be.

So what is the image of you that you have? Until this question is answered properly nothing can be resolved.

But yes this one fact stands out; the world dos not appreciate all the values that you have. This is the crux of existence. How to make others appreciate us? This is why

"BEING APPRECIATED" is such a big thing. It helps us value ourselves. Even false appreciation is ok.

Unknowingly we stand firm in our convictions and blame other for our ills. We are even prepared to lie and cheat as long as others see us in the good light we want to be seen. Often it is for short term profit but the hurt we do is long term. Just as revenge and anguish births in us we are doing our bit to birth it in others. As the population grows things are becoming cruelly complex as the number of people around us is growing and so are the demands. We are all of us pulling and kicking up each other's tailbones.

The arrows we unleash are flowing around us and not will sooner rather later come to hurt us. Humanity needs to understand now that there is no space for individual ivory towers. The good, the bad and the hurt to unleash will flow around you and you would too be its target. The emotions of revenge, envy and lust know no borders. Humans do tend to live in the illusion that life is = " I " & others. While I am perfect, virtuous, visionary the others are nincompoops, village urchins just out of their shells. Shatter this illusion yourself otherwise life will be forced to step in and this can be very painful indeed.

The added sting to this emotional warfare is the fact that our procreative energy is highly dependent on this appreciation factor. We cannot have sexual outings until the corresponding partner appreciates us enough to lower and do away with all the barriers…… And this is where all the pressures and problems begin and mount in human affairs.

Mother Nature has really swindled us into this state of affairs. Our need to be appreciated, to have sex also happens to be the Creative Force that makes us great. This brings the poet out in us and all the lovingness that we are capable of.

But again this selfish side in us does not make us good sociable beings and we throw about our actions and reactions, our resentments and bickering around with great abandon. We have to prove ourselves don't we? This is causing so much strife and anguish. The study of how humans force themselves on others just to prove to themselves that they are a "somebody" can be an eye opener into our dirty secrets of our beings.

It hurts to acknowledge but nobody really needs us. We may be useful to many and they would surely see that much at least so we stay together; but none really needs us. This is a sobering fact that is the foundation of a happy contented life.

Many individuals saw through this machination of Mother Nature. Behavioral rules were advised. Protocols of behavior were laid down. But instead of helping humanity it only curtailed their basic instinctive nature and created more frustrations and anguish. It also gave us Religions and more reasons for strife amongst us.

When we have lived long enough, we may out of fatigue sit down some time and reflect on the life we have had. We all do this one way or the other. We replay the moments and unwittingly we give birth to anguish in us. The unfulfilled dreams, the opportunities that we did not know how to profit from, the errors we made, the stupidities we committed, the stories that we cannot tell, the harm done to us that we cannot forgive……all these are hovering around us at all times and we pile up more anguish as we go along.

Quite obviously comes to us the next question: How do we reduce this burden of anguish?

The answer could be childishly simple:

Reduce the expectation quotient.

Appreciate genuinely.

Look at your own follies and see the same follies in action in others; specially the "Being Clever" element.

Then never forget. You really don't belong here on earth. You will be leaving like all others before you. What the hell are you so lathering about?

On the plus side I can vouch that we all get to be "Queen of the Spring Fair" at least for a short while in our lives. Be content with that and live away your life unconcerned with what others may be thinking about you. And please leave others alone to their demons.

We all have to live with our demons. It is a lonesome journey. Once we accept this and re-evaluate our lives with this in regard, contentment comes.

Haribol Acharya

Sometimes I wonder why people become corrupt. Few persons resist themselves from corruptions. Some people are corrupt just because they have the opportunity to be corrupt. There are others who are not corrupt just because they had no chance or opportunity to be corrupt. Those who can say outright no to corruption are very few in number. Whether we agree or not to accept the fact that very few can live a corruption free life.

Pradeep Pk Maheshwari

Conclusion: We are basically corrupt. A vessel for the Rakhshas forces. In the beginning we are relatively clean but environment like the home we are born into, the school we go to, the society we live start creating a nucleus of a doorway through which Forces find outlet.

They begin with small episodes and slowly as they find no resistance they establish themselves in the person and become the person.

This is why you will notice that every one of us has small fixed predictable persona. Others who are sensitive can feel it; the intelligent ones can see it.

Very few people see this in themselves so they become puppets to other forces and influences and go thru life like automatons.

Some people collect and collect cash with no idea what to do with it. They have no desire to spend it and dont even know what they want. But they keep on taking and taking as if hungry.

There are many of us getting angry at most unimportant things as if we can communicate only in anger. Others hurt others as if to see if they are truly alive and living on this earth and need to see others howling for effect. This is our sadistic side that loves to see others under our control.

Why women fall into the clutches of BAD men?

Firstly their own hormones are looking for outlets. These hormones are designed to select the most strong and healthy looking/smelling (pheromones) males. Mother Nature has only one interest – the propagation of the species. Unfortunately these males are generally low on the IQ or EQ side too. (This is why I advise to wait till one is nearer thirty. Till that age flirt but do not get attached/involved)

The education about life is sketchy and incomplete for which we need to blame the parenting. The education is mainly in the most opposite direction of playing it safe with understanding and circumspection.

Secondly to all the above we can add the basic nature of the ego in the female. It all begins by the feeling of being "NEEDED" This does them in. Males are good actors. They need the women so badly that are ever ready to grovel, submit to all infamy, go to long lengths to satisfy all whims and wishes of the women. Women are so pleased by all this that they are "sold". Sentences like "You are my dream come true", "You are ravishingly beautiful", "I don't think I am good enough for you", "You are astounding in so many ways" spurt the vanity to accept the male's overtures.

Women do put up a few tests and men who pass them are given whatever they want.

This is the trap. Very difficult to get out of it and even one realizes that one is trapped, often our pride does not accept it and we continue to believe that things will change or we can change the human with love and such other nonsensical thinking.

Don't tell me later that I did not warn you.

THE OTHER SIDE OF THE COIN

A labourer sold his daughter for Rs 30000. When asked why he said that that was the going rate for girls.

This is the problem when there are buyers, sellers will appear.

Sociologists may cry hoarse that this is immoral and against God and what not.

But reality is that girls are expressly being given birth for "selling".

This is the great LOVE that these "humans" talk of. Charlatans totally.

A lady I know got engaged to be married with great ceremony. She had known the man for 10 years. She insisted. But then something soured after the engagement. There was some talk of dowry. All LOVE flew out of the window. The engagement was broken. The family showed great courage in breaking off because the insult in society is seen as great.

The problem is in the false appearances we support. The insults we perceive.

Once a manufacturer came to my office to discuss exports. He had a young lady in tow. Her presence put me off. But I watched as my partner discussed. But the behaviour of the man was offending to me as he was treating us as if we didn't matter and that he was the man in control so self-assuredly.

I got annoyed and asked him to leave immediately. My partner was deeply annoyed with me because that man was offering the young lady as compensation for the export order and my partner so wanted it.

Women too have been quietly involved in selling themselves; have talked to many. They say how does it matter? It brings in great wealth without much effort. They forget that youth lasts only for some years and then it is the trash can. OR perhaps they know this well and make hay while the sun shines.

You want to learn to be happy?

Then look closely at the human race.

The human race on earth today has mastered the art of being unhappy. Specially these faculties: Faking it, Imagining it, Pretending it, Wasting it, Sulking it, Scoffing it, laughing it off, Waving it off as unimportant and Unseeing it.

All the diametrically OPPOSITE ways are the secret to happiness.

YES. Look how we exalt the Chimera.

We all know deep down that it is as untruthful as the image we project of ourselves. When we wish to avoid talking of ourselves we deliberately choose some other subject. Earlier it was the weather; now it is the screen personas and virtual reality.

It is a good way of being seemingly involved without liabilities.

When we look at these manufactured celebrities from the film or for that matter any industry we are really looking at what we feel we are too and stand alongside. Had the circumstances of birth been different we are no less. Anyway we show our alignment with the images they conjure.

It is all the technology and lifestyle that has built-up around us that has created a "weakness" syndrome in our entire physiological make-up and less tolerant mentally.

We are now thinking in terms of vaccines and antibiotics, concrete and insulation to protect ourselves. The body is losing its ability to fight its own wars as there is really no need to develop its defenses.

We want now and expect a regulated and thermostatically environment 24x7x365; always well fed with choicest and preferred food alone and no ups and downs in anything even relationships. We expect to be understood and amused at all times with the world moving and behaving in line with our moods and preferences.

We are manufacturing garbage individually and collectively + industrially which has to "BE" on this same planet - where do you think the dirt will go? IT IS BOUND to come back to us.

We are not victims; we are the perpetrators.

....

Author: Pradeep PK Maheshwari; From Sri Aurobindo
Ashram, Pondicherry. India.

Life time work: Country manager for European Companies.
Consumer products Design Consultant. Internationally
exposed to Trading, Teaching & Counseling, Marketing,
Technical Joint ventures, Travel Trade/Tourism. Speak:
French and English, Hindi. Deep interest in healing thru
Homeopathy, Naturopathy and very particularly
Orthomolecular Therapy.

Hobbies - Writing, photography, painting, product
development.

Teaching and counseling have been my activities in
association with many institutions in Delhi.